# spiritual realities

## Volume 1

# THE SPIRITUAL WORLD
# AND
# HOW WE ACCESS IT

by

Harold R. Eberle

**Spiritual Realities Volume I:**
**The Spiritual World and How We Access It**

Copyright © 1997

**Winepress Publishing**
**P.O. Box 10653**
**Yakima, WA 98909-1653**
**1-800-308-5837**

Library of Congress Catalog Card No. 97-060374
ISBN 1-882523-07-5

Cover by Jeff Boettcher
Graphic Art by Diane Buchanan and Eugene M. Holmes

All Biblical quotations are taken from the *New American Standard Bible*
© 1977, The Lockman Foundation, La Habra, California 90631.

# Dedication and Thanks

This book would not have been possible if it had not been for Pastor Jim Leuschian of Spokane, Washington, who helped me think through the many doctrinal issues and challenged me on numerous points. His theological insight brought me back down to earth and forced me to communicate spiritual principles in understandable terms.

Also, I had input and editing advice from R. E. McMaster, Ken Kolman, Martha Brookhart, Peter Eisenmann, John Frady, and Dennis Jacobson. Annette Bradley deserves special mention for her expertise in the area of editing and preparing the final copy. Each of these have left their mark on these pages and on my life.

However, I owe most to my staff who have faithfully given their time month by month and served in love over the last five years: Linda (my wife), Mike and Maria Clark, Mike and Maribel Pillsbury, Shane and Barbara Donaldson, Dave and Diane Buchanan, Tad and Michele Romberger, and Ken and Robbie Kolman. I ask the people who read these words to pray for my staff, their marriages, children, lives and walks with God.

# Table of Contents

# Introduction

⟨Remove the supernatural from Christianity and you no longer have Christianity.⟩ Without the spiritual and miraculous aspects recorded in the Bible, you have very few pages left of the Holy Book. Still, many Christians deny present-day experiences related to the spiritual world. Or at best, they are defensive and fearful about the supernatural realm, not wanting to talk about it and warning everyone to stay away.

At the same time, the general population is intrigued with spiritual realities. Popular television programs are incorporating supernatural phenomena and paranormal experiences into the lives of their actors. The New Age Movement, which emphasizes the spiritual dimension in an anti-Christian context, is spreading at a phenomenal rate worldwide. Young people surrounding us are being reared on videos portraying every aspect pertaining to the invisible dimension. Occult and various mystical teachings are a part of their daily diets. The world is paying money to witness mystical phenomena which is reported in magazines and portrayed in our movie theaters. This should tell us something, since Jesus said that where a person's money is, there is his heart. People give themselves to these things because they are hungry for spiritual reality.

# The Spiritual World and How We Access It

It is time for the Church to offer God's answers to the people around us who are hungering. We must not allow evil men and women to fill the void. It is not enough for Christians to give warnings concerning this cult or that deception. Our Christian bookstores have volumes and volumes written on the dangers associated with the New Age groups, and those warnings should be taken seriously. However, our whole outlook must change. So long as we are on the defensive, we will not win this generation to our Lord Jesus Christ. We do not need another writing cautioning us to stay away from evil powers. We must get on the offensive.

Most importantly, it is time that we prepare the Church for an increase of the supernatural in Her midst. I am writing with a belief that God is beginning to move in new power among His people. In the past, we have seen various gifts of the Holy Spirit, but it is our hope and faith that before the return of Jesus Christ, the Church will arise to a place of maturity, during which She will do the very works of Jesus, and greater works (John 14:12). We will, indeed, see God move in power, showing signs and wonders that previously have not been seen in the earth.

It is time that Christians understand and learn how to experience the supernatural in a greater measure. One of the most outstanding features we see in the lives of the men and women in the Bible is the spiritual phenomena that accompanied them. Just as Moses shamed Pharaoh's magicians, so also Christians should be able to demonstrate the power of God and shame the mystics and false prophets of our days. We do not need to be warned about evil as

2

much as we need to be taught about God's power. Since the kingdom of light is greater than all darkness, it is time we rise up to a higher level of spiritual awareness and tap into that which God is offering to us.

Our textbook will be the Bible. The Bible is the most comprehensive and accurate book that reveals how the spiritual world influences us. By using it, we can come to a clearer understanding of spiritual dynamics than by reading all the occult and New Age books that ever have been published. The answers for which people are seeking are right there in the Book of all books.

In order to cover all the necessary information, we have had to divide our teachings into seven volumes. It is difficult to separate the individual topics, because the information presented in the earlier volumes is needed to fully understand later materials. We know that some readers will be tempted to jump ahead and investigate areas of particular interest, but we do not want you to misunderstand later truths which depend upon points made earlier. Please keep in mind that this entire set is written in a progressive manner, building one truth upon another.

The various volumes of this book are written so they can be studied either by an individual or taught in a group setting.

It is my belief that Christians are hungry to learn about the spiritual world. Every time I have taught on this subject to various Christian groups, the response has been shockingly favorable. People have many unanswered questions in this area because we have not talked about them openly.

# The Spiritual World and How We Access It

In the Old Testament times among the Jewish people, there were various "Schools of the Prophets." No one knows for sure what actually was studied in such gatherings, but certainly those with spiritual inclinations learned much about the workings of God and the invisible world. We hope this book will be of similar value, but we call this the "School of the Spirit." Welcome to class!

# Developing a Picture of
# the Spiritual World

The prophet Elisha once prayed for his servant, saying, "O Lord, I pray, open his eyes that he may see" (II Kings 6:17). The servant's spiritual eyes then were opened and he beheld horses and chariots of fire all around them. What the servant could not have seen previously in the world of the spirit, God allowed him to see, and he was amazed.

What if we prayed the prayer of Elisha and God answered by opening our eyes? What would the spiritual world around us look like? If the walls disappeared and the ceiling vanished, and then our eyes beheld the angels and demons and the entire invisible world surrounding us, what is it we would see right now?

Through the following pages we hope to develop an understanding of that world. Many people have had various spiritual experiences and witnessed supernatural phenomena. If we desire to talk about these and understand for ourselves what is true and what is false, we can begin our study by developing an accurate picture of the spiritual world, based upon what we are shown in the Bible.

## The Spiritual World and How We Access It

First of all, we must note that the spiritual world is *another world.* It is not merely an imaginary dimension or the invisible part of the natural world. Hebrews 11:3 tells us that the natural world was made out of that which is invisible. Therefore, the spiritual world must be greater than the entire universe, since it existed before this natural world. We understand that it overlaps and envelops our natural world.

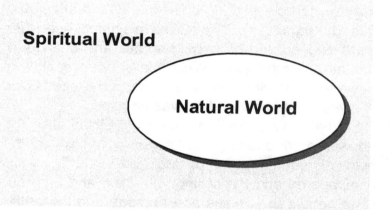

**Spiritual World**

**Natural World**

In our diagram above we have shown the spiritual world surrounding the natural world, however, we do not want to imply that the natural world is small or that the two dimensions are separated from each other. It is best to envision the natural world as superimposed upon the invisible, spiritual world. Both worlds are big — perhaps with no outer boundaries. We draw the natural world within the spiritual simply to show that the spiritual world pre-exists and supersedes the natural world.

# Developing a Picture of the Spiritual World

The spiritual realm is where God dwells. Jesus said, "God is spirit, and those who worship Him must worship in spirit and truth" (John 4:24).

The spiritual world is also where angels exist. When we talk about angels, do not think just of pretty white creatures floating around on wings. The Bible describes some beautiful angels with wings (i.e., Isaiah 6:2; Exodus 25:20), but there are also spiritual creatures which are powerful, and terrifying for any human even to see. For example, the prophet Ezekiel was allowed to see the four living beings in the world of the spirit, each having four faces: that of a man, that of a lion, that of a bull, and that of an eagle (Ezek. 1:4-21). As these living beings moved together, lightning flashed round about them and the sight was terrifying to Ezekiel. Such beings exist in the world of the spirit, and we must keep in mind that creatures like these and others described in the Bible (i.e., the Book of Revelation), are not demons, but spiritual creatures on God's side.

In the spiritual world there are two kingdoms, God's and Satan's (Col. 1:13; Acts 26:18). God's kingdom is referred to in the Bible as the kingdom of light, and it is ruled by Jesus Christ, who is sitting on a throne at the right hand of God the Father. Satan's kingdom is the dominion of darkness, and many devils are under Satan's evil influence there. We must not envision these two kingdoms as being on an equal level of authority or power. Jesus has been exalted far above all rule and authority (Eph. 1:20-22). Satan is merely a created being. Jesus is one with the Father, co-Creator and eternal.

# Spiritual World

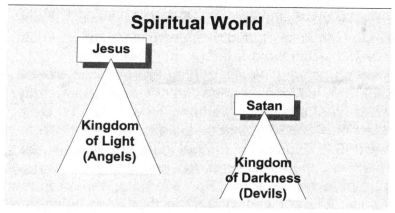

There are many other *things* in the spiritual world. In using the word *things,* we are not talking about material elements made of physical substance, but rather things of spiritual substance, invisible to us, but indeed real. In Ephesians 1:3, we are told that God "has blessed us with every spiritual blessing in the heavenly places in Christ." We understand that God has prepared many blessings which are awaiting those who love Him. More than that, we understand that whatever God ever has thought or spoken in the spiritual world has come into existence there. Just like this world has real things made of natural substances, such as rock, water and wood, so also the spiritual world has things of spiritual substance. It is, in fact, a world full of unseen treasures.

It is equally as important for us to realize that the laws which govern the spiritual world are different from those which govern the natural world. For example, in the natural world there is a law of gravity. In the spiritual world, there is no such law and, therefore, spirit entities can "fly," if we want to call it that; or at the least they can move about freely without physical limitations.

This subject gets a little mystical when we start talking about distance and space in the spiritual realm. Some people wrongly have said that there is neither space nor distance in the spirit. That, however, is not true. It would be more accurate to say that there is space, but spirit entities are not limited by it, as we are in the natural world.

This point is important for our later discussions and, therefore, we must establish it in our minds clearly. We know there is space, because Satan is not in all places at all times. In the book of Job, chapter 1, we read of how Satan spoke to God, telling Him that he had been roaming about upon the earth. Satan does not fill the earth; rather, he is limited in his location to one place at a time. The fact that Satan first had to go *into* the throne room of God in order to talk to the Lord, implies that distance and location have some meaning in the spiritual world.

Though distance and space are realities there, the limits are not the same as we experience on this earth. Of course, spirit entities can move about freely, but also consider the following Bible passage. In Luke 8:26-39, we read about an incident when our Lord Jesus cast a legion of demons out of a certain man. A *legion* in that day referred to a huge multitude, even several thousand. Since we are told that a legion of demons came out of the man, we can ask the question, "How many demons actually can fit into a human vessel?" Obviously, size and space in the spiritual world have different meanings than those to which we are accustomed in this natural world.

*spatial—*
*relating to space*

## The Spiritual World and How We Access It

Still, we do not want to deny spatial relationships. In fact, there are correlations in this respect between the spiritual world and the natural. Think back to when Elisha's servant was allowed to see the fiery chariots. Those chariots, we are told, were *on the mountain* (II Kings 6:17). Indeed, we see many such relationships in the Bible between natural mountains and spiritual positions of authority; for example, God met Moses on Mount Sinai. Jacob beheld a ladder at a certain location, upon which angels ascended and descended (Gen. 28:10-17). Even the fact that devils seek to inhabit a human vessel implies their attachment to locations.

*location*

At this point, what we need to understand on this subject is that there are places of light and darkness, both in the spiritual world and in the natural world. At times there may be a correlation between these. The spiritual world is not a homogeneous mass of good and bad. No. There are *hot spots* and *cold spots*. There are places that are holy and some that are desecrated. When the spiritual world overlaps this natural world, there are often correlations between what is happening in the two worlds.

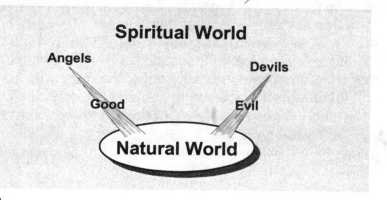

**Spiritual World**

Angels

Devils

Good

Evil

**Natural World**

Finally, we want to identify one other law and its significance in the spiritual world. This law has to do with time. In the natural world, tomorrow follows today, and all is progressing at a uniform rate. As we have stated, the laws that govern the spiritual world are different from the laws that govern the natural world. In relation to time, this is very important.

Do not make the mistake which some have made and assume that time does not exist in the spiritual world. That is not true. *Time does exist.* If it did not, then Satan would know all things, the beginning and the end. We are told in the Bible that God will one day throw Satan into the Lake of Fire, where he "will be tormented day and night forever and ever" (Rev. 20:10). If some restrictions were not imposed upon the spiritual world, devils would simply escape God's judgment and move into another time period. The fact is that devils are limited in time, even though they exist in the spiritual world.

Equally significant is the fact that things in the spiritual realm are changing. For example, two thousand years ago Jesus ascended far above all rule and authority. If time did not exist in the spiritual realm, devils could not be rebelling at one point, and then be subjected to our Lord's authority at another point. If time did not exist, nothing could change in that world.

Time does exist in the spiritual world. We do not know whether time always has existed, or whether it started "in the beginning." All we know for sure is that time now is both in the natural world and in the spiritual world.

**11**

## The Spiritual World and How We Access It

Having said all that, we also must point out that God transcends both time and space. He is the Creator. He does not change (Mal. 3:6). Jesus, Who is co-Creator, declared Himself as the Alpha and the Omega, the beginning and the end. From God's perspective, all things stand before Him to see and know. He is the *I Am* at all times.

With this basic understanding, we can go on to study man's relationship to the spiritual world — how we influence it and how it influences us. Many of the spiritual phenomena we need to discuss only can be explained as we develop a Biblically accurate view of the spiritual world. As we continue, we will learn how Christians may perceive things in the spiritual dimension. In addition, they may be allowed by God to experience or change various things belonging to other places and times. We also will see how Satan counterfeits these and many other such phenomena. By doing this, we hope to answer many questions which Christians have concerning the spiritual world.

# 2

## Our Contact With the Spiritual World

It is the Christian belief that people have more to their being than just a physical body. The Bible teaches us that we have a spirit/soul. Volume II of these studies is dedicated to explaining the functions and makeup of the spirit/soul of man. Without delving too far into the nature of man at this point, we just want to state now that the spirit of man exists in the spiritual realm. Just as the body is in direct contact with the natural world, the spirit is in direct contact with the spiritual world. Right now, while you are reading these words, you exist in two worlds at the same time. This is what the Christian faith declares, although many have not considered the implications.

**You exist in two worlds:**

## The Spiritual World and How We Access It

There is a stark difference between the Christian's and the non-Christian's experience of the spiritual world. Because of sin, there is a separation between God and the unregenerated person. When forgiveness is obtained through Jesus Christ, God opens the door for relationship.

Furthermore, the kingdom of God has been established within the spiritual world. The believer has access to that kingdom, for he has been transferred from the kingdom of darkness into the kingdom of light (Col. 1:13). The non-Christian has a spirit in contact with the spiritual world, and he can experience that dimension; but not the blessings of God therein, because "...unless a man is born again, he cannot see the kingdom of God" (John 3:3). Both the Christian and the non-Christian are influenced by the spiritual world; but there is a difference, in that the believer can communicate with and receive directly from God, Who is in that realm.

It is for this reason that when a non-Christian goes "into the spirit" (to be explained in the next chapter), he is exposing himself to evil. His spirit is an open door for demonic influences to work. In contrast, the Christian interacts with both God's and Satan's kingdom. We are told that *whatever he binds or looses will be bound or loosed* (Matt. 18:18-19). Of course, the believer can be influenced by evil and tempted by the devil, but he also has access to God's power and blessings.

This is what we want to identify here: how a person can sense things in the spiritual world. Our first point is this: Your spirit exists in the spiritual dimension, and, therefore, it is right now in contact with that world. Next, we want to explain how you have spiritual senses. Just as you have physical senses (i.e., hearing, sight, touch,...) to perceive what is occurring in the natural world, so also you have spiritual senses telling you what is happening in the spiritual world.

Some Christians never have been taught this truth. They do not realize that they already possess certain spiritual senses. I like to make it clear to them by asking, "Does the devil ever tempt you?" The obvious answer is, "Yes, the devil tempts everyone at some point." My next question, "How can you *hear* what the devil is saying?" The devil exists in the spiritual world. If you hear him, that means you have the ability to hear spiritual impressions. There is the proof that you have spiritual ears.

The fact is that every human being has been created with spiritual senses. The Bible gives us the proper understanding of these senses, indicating to us that we all have them, but they are not active or very receptive in most people. We see this in passages such as the one where Elisha prayed that his servant's spiritual eyes might be opened, so that he might see the angels gathered around (II Kings

6:17). Elisha did not pray that his servant would *receive* eyes but rather that the eyes he had would be *opened*. Similarly, in the New Testament Paul expressed his prayer that the eyes of the Christian's heart would be opened up (Eph. 1:18). Many Bible passages talk about the "ears" of some people being open to God while others are closed. It is not the *receiving* of these spiritual senses, but the *quickening* of them that people need.

The "quickening" of a person's spiritual senses can happen through the enablement of good or evil spirit beings. In Acts 16:16-18, we read about a woman who could foretell the future through the aid of *a spirit of divination*. This spirit communicating with the woman was a devil, which the Apostle Paul cast out of her.

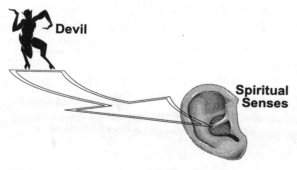

Devil

Spiritual Senses

There are also people whom God has super-naturally enabled to perceive things in the spiritual realm. For example, we are told of the Prophet Daniel:

> "... extraordinary spirit, knowledge
> and insight, interpretation of

dreams, explanation of enigmas, and solving of difficult problems were found in this Daniel..." (Dan. 5:12).

Of course, we know that it was the Holy Spirit who gifted Daniel in these ways. Similarly, the Spirit of God enabled many of those about whom the facts were reported in the New Testament to perceive and understand things in the spiritual dimension.

We do not want you to have the impression that only those who have "special gifts" are able to perceive realities of the spirit. Of course, there are some who will have special enablements through either demonic or God's empowering, but every human being has a spirit which exists in the spiritual world. It is always in contact with that world. Every human being was created with a spirit bearing spiritual sensitivities. The functioning of those senses is largely dependent upon an individual simply being receptive.

This "availability to all" is especially important for the Christian, because he has been transferred from the kingdom of darkness into the kingdom of light. The Holy Spirit desires to work in every believer's life revealing to him the will of God and the realities of His kingdom (I Cor. 2:10-13) Receiving things from the Holy Spirit is not just a possibility for *some* Christians, but the privilege of *all* Christians.

In the next chapter we will explain how the Christian can be receptive to that which comes to his spirit. In other words, we will discuss how a person can *tune in to* the things which his spirit is sensing in the spiritual world. Here, we simply want to establish the fact that communication is possible.

It seems strange to me, but many Christians today do not believe that God will communicate directly with men. The contradiction in that viewpoint is that the same Christians will talk about how they battle with certain temptations and how Satan is active in the world influencing men to do evil. They believe that the devil inspires his thoughts in the minds and hearts of men, but they do not think God is doing the same thing. To have more faith in the activity of Satan than in the work of God, is foolish and tragic.

When we talk about God speaking to the Christian, we usually are not referring to an audible voice coming from the sky. God can talk in that fashion, as He did several times in the Bible (i.e., Acts 9:4-7); however, we usually are speaking about how He inspires His thoughts and desires upon our conscious mind through the avenue of our spirit. The Apostle Paul explained it this way:

For to us God revealed them through the Spirit; for the Spirit searches all things, even the depths of God. For who among men knows the thoughts of a man except the spirit of the man, which is in him? Even so the thoughts of God no one knows except the Spirit of God. Now we have received, not the spirit of the world, but the Spirit who is from God, that we might know the things freely given to us by God (I Cor. 2:10-12).

We are told in this passage that the will and thoughts of God are made known to us through the Holy Spirit revealing things to our spirit. This is the primary avenue through which we can experience God.

Now, the communication which the Holy Spirit has with our spirit is not the same as our communication on the natural level with other human beings. Paul explained that spiritual truths only can be relayed in spiritual terms (I Cor. 2:7 & 13). The language and even the words which we have developed to talk with people in this world are inadequate to convey spiritual realities. In fact, our natural human thought patterns are not able to receive many of the spiritual truths God wants to communicate to us. For this reason, Paul explained in First Corinthians, chapter two, that the naturally-minded person, even if he is a Christian, cannot receive the things of the spirit. Spiritual thoughts can

**19**

only be communicated to those who are spiritually minded. Communication of spiritual realities must take place on the level of the spirit.

How, then, does the Holy Spirit communicate God's will to our spirits? Of course, there are times when God may use words and thought patterns familiar to our natural reasoning and training, but primarily He uses *spiritual impressions* upon our spirit. The Holy Spirit reveals the will of God to us through stirrings, nudges, words, spiritual pictures, burdens, and unctions. Ezekiel explained that the Spirit would work within us, *causing* us to do the Father's will (Ezek. 36:27). The Apostle Paul wrote that the Christian's spirit is "alive" (Rom. 8:10), meaning that our spirit is responsive and sensitive to God. It is as if the Holy Spirit were brushing against us or silently pushing us from within, according to the plans and purposes of God.

There is also a communication in the spirit which cannot even be explained with human understanding. We call it "revelation." A person simply "knows something." He does not know how he knows. He did not arrive at the understanding through experience, education, or logical reasoning. As a light shining from a projector onto a screen, so is the direction of God often revealed through the spirit and then reflected upon the conscious mind. Some would call this intuition, but that term gives no credit to the role God's Spirit may play. Of course, we are not saying that all intuitive knowledge is from God, but there is a real transmission of information that can take place directly from the Holy Spirit to a person's spirit.

Spiritual eyesight is also important in perceiving the spiritual world. As we pointed out, every human being has eyes to perceive things in the spirit. We are referring here to the images and pictures which arise within our mind. Proverbs 20:27 tells us, "The spirit of man is the lamp of the Lord...." Most people have a hard time distinguishing between their own imaginations and the functioning of their spiritual eyesight. Our experiences of the two are very similar. Both manifest as pictures upon the mind, but one originates from the spiritual world and the other within the person himself. The images which come through this form of spiritual communication are called *visions.*

Some visions come during the night while a person is asleep. The Bible plainly tells us that God speaks to us in dreams (Job 33:14-16). Of course, not all dreams are from God, and we will discuss the function of dreams in a later volume. Here we are simply adding this truth to our concept of God's communication with us.

These and other forms of spiritual communication all have a "spiritual nature" to them. As the spirit of a man originates from the breath of God, so also communication at that level has the qualities of a gentle breeze. Jesus explained,

> "The wind blows where it wishes and you hear the sound of it, but do not know where it comes from and where it is going; so is everyone who is born of the Spirit" (John 3:8).

## The Spiritual World and How We Access It

Like the blowing wind, so is the work of the Holy Spirit. Images, words, nudges, burdens, impressions, etc. — such are the workings of the Spirit as He acts upon and reveals things to the Christian's spirit.

Finally, we need to add that God communicates in many other ways. Here we simply are learning about the spiritual forms of communication. God also talks to people through the written Word, other people, circumstances, events, etc. We do not want to limit our thinking, but our intentions in this book are to focus upon and open to the world of the spirit.

With this understanding of communication on the spiritual level, we now can continue. As we do so, we will learn not only of spiritual phenomena in the Christian's life, but also in the lives of evil men and women. The spiritual communication that witches, mediums, channelers, New Age disciples, yogis, etc., practice and experience, all come in the form of spiritual impressions, images and stirrings. In this sense, the communication they receive is very much like that which a Christian receives. The most obvious difference, however, is the *source* of that communication from within the spiritual world.

obvious source of difference — communication

# How To Tune In to the Spirit

As we now explain how people can tune in to the world of the spirit, we are not giving credence to those who communicate with the dead or engage in spiritist activity or any other such evils. The Bible plainly warns us:

> "There shall not be found among you anyone...who uses divination, one who practices witchcraft, or one who interprets omens, or a sorcerer, or one who casts a spell, or a medium, or a spiritist, or one who calls up the dead. For whoever does these things is detestable to the Lord" (Deut. 18:10-12a; see also Is. 8:19-20).

Make no mistake about God's attitude toward these spiritual activities.

# The Spiritual World and How We Access It

What we will teach here is how Christians can access God and His blessings in the spiritual dimension. God has told us in several Bible verses that "if we seek Him with our whole heart and soul, then we will find Him" (i.e., Deut. 4:29). This *discovering* of God is not in the usual sense of God always being with the Christian every minute of every day. No. It is possible to seek God in such a way that He actually will reveal Himself to us and make Himself known.

When we talk about such issues, some people have immediate fears and reactions arise within them. They have wrongly accepted a view of our relationship with God as one in which we should be totally inactive and passive. They do not know if it is right for a Christian to take the initiative in seeking God. The truth is that many examples and exhortations are given to us in the Bible concerning our taking the initiative in the pursuit of God. We are assured that if we draw near to God, He will draw near to us (James 4:8). It was with great earnestness and drive that Moses sought God (Ex. 33:12-18). King David, we are told, often went and "inquired of the Lord." Prayer itself, which we are encouraged to do, is the activity of men attempting to communicate with God. The Bible very clearly instructs us to go boldly, without fear, into His throne room (Heb. 4:16). Yes, it is right for the Christian to seek God actively.

How, then, can we find Him?

God exists in the spiritual realm. Jesus declared, "God is spirit and those who worship Him must worship Him in spirit and truth" (John 4:24). This was stated in the context of our Lord talking with a certain

Samaritan woman. The woman asked Jesus about certain forms of worship — whether people should worship God on one mountain or another (John 4:20). She was focused upon natural aspects when worshipping. Jesus changed her focus from the natural to the spiritual, declaring that "God is spirit" — He exists in the spiritual realm. What is important, therefore, is that we worship God as He exists in that realm.

When God states that He is "spirit" and that we must worship Him "in spirit," He is taking the position that we must go into His realm to have contact with Him. I can compare this with my relationship with you right now. I live in the state of Washington in the U.S.A. If I said, "I am an American who lives in Washington," I would be stating my own residence. Then I could say, "If you want to talk to me, you will have to come to Washington." Of course, you can read the things I have written, but if you really want to talk to me, you will have to come to where I live. In the same way, God has stated His residence. He is spirit. Those who want to worship Him must go to where He is.

How then can we go there? Again, God told us that if we seek Him with our *whole being,* then we will find Him. What you and I must do is take our whole heart and aim it, direct it, focus it, point it, toward Him. The focus of our entire heart, soul, and mind is the requirement.

In the Old Testament we often read of King David going to inquire of the Lord. In Psalm 131 we read of the attitude of heart David had when he approached God:

**27**

> O Lord, my heart is not proud,
> nor my eyes haughty;
> Nor do I involve myself in great
> matters,
> Or in things too difficult for me.
> Surely I have composed and
> quieted my soul;
> Like a weaned child rests
> against his mother,
> My soul is like a weaned child
> within me (Ps. 131:1-2).

Notice, first and foremost, the calming of David's soul. David set aside all his natural concerns and took on an attitude of humility. In that state he approached God.

In the New Testament we are taught the same principles. James tells us that as we draw near to God, He draws near to us (4:8). He described in that context how we are to draw near by separating ourselves from the concerns of the world (vs. 1-4), humbling ourselves (vs. 5-6), submitting to Him (vs. 7), and then cleansing our hearts (vs. 8). James also told us not to be "double-minded" when we come to God, because our thoughts must be fixed upon Him.

Now, some Christians may be confused by this teaching because they have been taught that God is always with the Christian, and no process or steps need to be taken to approach Him. Of course, God receives His children on the basis of their being forgiven and cleansed through Jesus Christ. God hears the prayers of His children, and He always wants us to talk to Him. In addition, the human spirit always exists in the realm of the spirit, and as we explained, God always is willing to communicate with the Christian.

However, it is also true that we must come before God and make ourselves sensitive to Him. We, by an act of our will, must open ourselves to receive from Him in a determined approach, in order to encounter and experience Him in a fuller way. Jesus Himself abides within the Christian's spirit, but as a person directs his attention toward God, he becomes more conscious of Him. His soul comes into agreement with God. The body becomes filled with the nature of God as it fulfills its function as a temple of the Holy Spirit. God's presence is *manifested* to the entire being of the believer as he draws nearer to the Father.

Look again at the exhortation in James 4:1-10, concerning how we may draw near to God. After explaining how we must separate ourselves from this natural world, put on humility and cleanse our souls, the writer says,

> Be miserable and mourn and weep; let your laughter be turned into mourning, and your joy to gloom. Humble yourselves in the presence of the Lord, and He will exalt you (James 4:9-10).

The opening of the door to God's presence here is preceded by the instructions to "be miserable and mourn and weep." We do not want to give the impression that communication with God is only possible if a Christian takes on a sorrowful attitude,

**29**

but we do need to recognize why this exhortation to "be miserable and mourn" is included here.

In the modern-day Church, we often emphasize the elements of rejoicing and grace so much that many Christians cannot understand the significance of sadness as an attitude of heart and mind helpful in seeking God. Of course, most of the daily Christian life should be exciting and joyful; but pursuing God in the spirit is an entirely different issue, and weeping does have an important function.

Mourning produces within the individual a brokenness necessary for a person's heart to be receptive to that which God wants to reveal. It calms the soul so God's thoughts can be heard. It positions the heart in humility before Him. Also, the act of mourning causes a separation of one's being from everything foreign clinging to it. By this we mean that all the cares of the world and desires for other things exert a force upon people which holds them back from God. Mourning redirects the soul and allows it to break free of those things which hinder it from fully focusing upon God (II Cor. 7:10-11).

## The Function of Mourning:

**Seeking God**

Natural and emotional attachments

*mourning produces brokenness*

*Sorrowing will produce according to God a repentance.*

30

The more a Christian gets in touch with God by calming his soul and focusing upon the spirit, the easier it becomes for him. The man who is intensely wrapped up in his business may have a difficult time setting it all aside. The mother who is worried about all the various concerns of her life will have a hard time calming her soul enough to receive from God. The person who has all his soul locked onto the natural realm may have a battle redirecting his attention. Each time a person successfully comes before God, it establishes pathways in the spirit in the same fashion that a person who repeatedly tries to do a natural job finds it easier and easier.

The process of opening oneself up to the spirit can be aided in several ways. For example, fasting (that is, not eating food for a time) may help a person deny his body and detach from physical desires and the natural concerns of life. Music can be a great benefit by creating a spiritual atmosphere in which a person easily can forget things and calm his soul. It was for this reason that the prophets in the Old Testament would sometime call a minstrel, so that they could begin to hear from God and speak His words (II Kings 3:15). At other times men of God would separate themselves, putting some distance between them and all other people. In similar fashion, Christians may find themselves more able to receive from God during an extended time, isolated alone in a quiet place of prayer. Simply relaxing and calming the soul in a very natural setting also can open a person to the spirit.

Though we mention these outward conditions, the real focus of our understanding must be upon the heart of man. When a person takes his heart, turns it away from the things of this world, and directs it completely toward God, then God will reveal Himself. God declared that He is a jealous God (Ex. 20:5; see also James 4:5). It is for this reason that He holds the greatest revelations of Himself for those who seek Him with *all of their heart.* In that condition, a person may find himself losing interest in the natural things and even "hating" them in a sense (Luke 14:26), as those natural things lose all importance when compared with finding God. As Moses cried out for God to reveal Himself, he said:

> "If Thy presence does not go
> with us, do not lead us up from
> here" (Ex. 33:15).

Moses had come to the point of not wanting even to go on unless God would reveal Himself. In this sense, an individual may come to the point of wanting "nothing but God" in their pursuit of Him. Only when a person has come to such a point of focus has he completely turned his heart away from other things and onto Him.

At the start of seeking God, Christians may find their attention focusing on all kinds of natural concerns, needs, desires or other people. They have not turned their heart completely toward God until all those things and people fade into insignificance. They only have detached in heart from those things *when they no longer desire to go back to them.* Gradually, and then suddenly, a change occurs when their heart completely turns, and then *they want to stay in the presence of God.*

As soon as the conscious mind and the heart of a person are focused upon the spirit, the senses begin to receive that with which he is in contact spiritually. Now, we have been talking about encountering God and the kingdom of God, but it is important to understand that our spiritual senses can open to the whole spiritual dimension. God is not the only one out there. It also is the home of devils and the kingdom of which they are a part. So also, the spirits of all men exist in that dimension. Forces which influence the future, along with an unlimited number of other spiritual "things," can be encountered. We want you to realize that an entire spiritual world is out there, but we do not want you to conclude that an individual can decide sovereignly what to explore or encounter. In later volumes, we explain more clearly the various aspects of the spiritual world which people experience.

In the Book of Revelation, we read of how the Apostle John was "in the spirit" one day (Rev. 1:10); and hence, his spiritual eyes opened to see all about which he described in the rest of the book. John wrote about angels, devils, the sins of several churches, coming judgment, people who would walk upon the earth in the last days, and many, many other spiritual realities. In the Book of Acts we can read about the Prophet Agabus who knew by the spirit what the future held in store for Paul (Acts 21:10-11). On another occasion, Paul's spirit within him was sensing demonic influences over the city of Athens (Acts 17:16). When a person's spiritual senses are receptive, he may become aware of any of these entities, along with a multitude of other things.

## The Spiritual World and How We Access It

In coming chapters we will explain how to discern that which is received in the spirit and how to keep oneself in the Spirit of God. Here simply we are teaching how one *tunes in to the spirit* or *goes into the spirit.*

When a person goes "entirely" into the spirit, his conscious thought is directed completely toward that which is coming in through his spirit. The Apostle John was in this state when he saw all that he reported in the Book of Revelation (Rev. 1:10).

When God begins to reveal Himself to a believer, an endless number of things can occur. Very commonly, the presence of God flows through the spirit of the man, and then floods his soul and even his body in some measure. At that time God may impart strength, extra grace, answers to prayers, physical healing, victory over some sin, anointings, etc. He may reveal His desires, the future, revelations, or as Paul said, "Things which eye has not seen and ear has not heard..." (I Cor. 2:9-10). All of these things may flow from the Holy Spirit through the spirit of the person seeking God. Most importantly though, the believer may encounter God Himself in a very real, tangible sense.

Many Christians never have been taught these truths. They may have experienced God in some measure during a worship service, or a time alone, or in their ongoing daily lives. We praise God for those encounters, but here we are teaching a much fuller revelation that is available and possible for everyone who will seek God with their whole being. Moses saw God to the degree he was able. The curtain was torn through the death of Jesus Christ. Now all believers can go and see Him and know Him, to whatever degree they are willing.

With this foundational truth, we now can go on. Before we do, we want you to identify the state of one's being as he becomes sensitive to the spiritual realm. For a Christian to have his spiritual sensitivities turned on, he will find that he must detach from this world and direct his mind and heart completely toward God. Of course, God could and does reveal Himself at other times. However, the Bible also instructs us how to seek God in this fashion: detached from the natural concerns of life and completely focused upon Him.

*to whatever degree they are willing*

*must detach from this world and direct mind and heart completely toward God.*

# How Evil Spiritists
## Tap into the Spirit Realm

To help us understand what it means to tap into the spirit, I want to give some examples from natural life and from evil practices being used today. Cautions rise in my heart at this point because *I do not want you to misunderstand.* Some readers may wonder why I even would mention evil practices being used by witches, clairvoyants, psychics, New Agers, and others who worship false gods. Please allow me to explain.

When we refer to various evil spiritual exercises it most assuredly is not to promote them. Instead, our first and foremost goal is to answer the questions in Christian's hearts. Many Christians have been exposed to various occult practices at some time in their lives. The exposure may have occurred before they came to know Jesus personally, or they simply may have heard of evil activities and forms of witchcraft in the world. Other Christians are faced with the related problems because in their personal ministries they deal with people who are so involved. Many God-fearing parents even are finding that their children are being exposed to (or some other loved one actually is engaged in), witchcraft or New Age experiences. We cannot hide from the needs of those around us. We do not want to glorify or focus upon evil in any way, /but/ we must provide God's answers and equip believers to set people free.

My second reason for sharing some of the examples of evil practices is because they help people understand what actually is taking place in the spiritual realm and how it relates to man. Satan counterfeits the truth. He perverts it. He did not create man nor the spiritual realm. He merely is usurping authority and using spiritual principles which God created and ordained. When we mention a certain activity of those involved in evil spiritual practices, it should stir in us an expectancy to see what God has in that area that is greater.

My third reason for sharing some of the practices involved in witchcraft and various occult expressions is to expose the nakedness of all such evil. You see, there has developed around the various evil mystical experiences *an air of power*. Witches work hard to present an image of themselves as mysterious and powerful. The New Age advocates project the image that they have some hidden truth that belongs only to the elite of their bunch. Many Christians today are threatened by this whole image projected by the spiritists. They wonder what witches actually can and cannot do. Not knowing how to tap into God's power, they somehow feel inferior, at least in the spiritual dimension. Whether Christians admit it or not, many of them are fearful and defensive simply because they have been deceived by the mystical air projected by the occultists. Furthermore, they inwardly wonder whether they are missing out on something by being a Christian who diligently and faithfully keeps himself from even thinking about what the evil workers are doing.

I want Christians to know the truth. ⟨Being a Bible-believing Christian who is aware of the spiritual dimension, I personally have found that into which the Holy Spirit desires to lead us is far beyond — in glory and magnificence — anything that the New Agers or witches have⟩ I am not just saying this by faith. I know it to be true. The Bible not only gives us more accurate information, but also knowledge of the God who created it all. Because believers recognize that all authority comes from God, they do not need to suffer, as witches typically do, in their exercise of power (to be explained in a later volume). The Christian who truly taps into God's fullness has no less power or authority. In fact, he can far exceed that of which the evil workers partake.

Understanding this perspective, please allow me to discuss briefly, now and in later chapters, some of the spiritual practices performed by evil people.

For example, consider the witch who gazes into her crystal ball. Why does she do that? A witch does not see anything in the crystal ball; however, the large piece of glass serves as a focal point for her attention. As she stares into the glass, she can fix her mind, detach from the natural world, and begin to receive spiritual information. You probably have experienced a similar phenomenon when sitting by a campfire and staring into the open flame. Soon your mind fixates, the world around you is forgotten, and you are drifting in your imaginations. Some of those imaginations will arise from within yourself, but some others may be carried along by spiritual influences. It is in this fashion that a witch stares into her crystal ball, not because there is anything spiritual within it, but because it serves as a focal point.

It is with a similar purpose that some spiritists use small crystals. Staring into a crystal can cause their mind to detach from natural concerns. Having many crystals suspended on strings in a room can create an environment that seems mystical.

In the same way, idols, such as those carved out of wood or stone, may serve as objects upon which people can focus their attention. Indeed, as people sit quietly focused upon any such object, there is a feeling of detachment, and their spirit may begin to receive spiritual information from the other world.

As I share these things, again let me say that I am not encouraging Christians to engage in any such behavior. What we want you to see are the spiritual principles involved. Indeed, witches go into the spirit, and it requires a detachment from the natural world. They cannot experience the kingdom of God or His blessings; however, they may, indeed, tap into some spiritual influence. We as Christians may go into the spirit through the seeking of God with our whole soul and with all of our heart. However, we do not use what I like to call "illegal avenues of entrance." For example, God does not want us having idols molded with hands or made in any spiritual image. God declared:

"You shall not make for yourself
an idol, or any likeness of what

is in heaven above or on the
earth beneath or in the water
under the earth. You shall not
worship them or serve them; for
I the Lord your God, am a
jealous God..." (Ex 20:4-5).

We, as believers, must not put anything between us
and God. It is Him we must seek and worship.
    We also can talk about the use of rhythmic
music, chanting, or movement. Whenever a pattern
is repeated over and over, the mind will tend to block
it out and, simultaneously, block out other information
coming in from the natural world. Therefore, yoga
practitioners chant their mantras hour after hour.
Mystics rock back and forth until their minds are
drifting. New Agers will listen to rhythmic music that
causes their soul to quiet within them, and hypnotists
may swing a pendulum in front of their patient.
    Now, as a Christian, we must not condemn
categorically all rhythmic patterns. Otherwise, we
would have to reject the grandmother who prays
every night while relaxing in her rocking chair. We
also would need to condemn the mother who sings to
her baby while rocking her in the cradle. Obviously,
rhythmic patterns are not evil. In fact during church
services Christians should at times be encouraged to
sing songs again and again until they have laid aside
their natural concerns. Indeed, rhythmic music and
movement can be of help to people who are trying to
focus their attention upon God.
    However, as Christians who recognize spiritual
operations, we would warn people that rhythmic
patterns can open one's spirit to receive spiritual

**41**

influences that are not good. The hypnotized person may be yielding his will to spirit entities or to the will of the hypnotist. The mantras that spiritual trainees are instructed to repeat may be foreign words giving worship to false gods. The people with whom an individual relaxes may impart spiritual influences into that person's being, while together they open their spirits (this will be explained more fully in later volumes). It is not the rhythmic movement or rhythmic sounds that we reject, but the opening of one's spirit without discernment or recognition of evil.

It is with a much more critical eye that we must talk about those who use various drugs to enter the spiritual world. It is common, among primitive peoples in third-world countries, for certain individuals to act as witch doctors or medicine men. Often their practices include putting themselves in hallucinatory states of mind by smoking or ingesting certain mushrooms, drugs, or other plant products. Indeed, they may tap into the spiritual world, but using forbidden means and having no knowledge of the true God, they open themselves to an unlimited number of evil spiritual influences.

The use of drugs, however, is not limited to primitive peoples. There are some in our modern society using their own concoctions to experience the other world. Without knowing it, some are opening their spirit to the spiritual dimension through the use of cocaine, LSD, heroin, marijuana, and even alcohol. Not all abuses of such drugs result in spiritual experiences, but the possibility of detaching from the natural realm and yielding to the other side is always there.

## How Evil Spiritists Tap into the Spirit Realm

Even more blatantly evil are the practices of witches and warlocks carried out in their secretive meetings and black masses. A mystical atmosphere may be set up in an isolated environment. Incense may captivate the sense of smell. Eerie music may lure a participant into a spiritual consciousness. Drugs can release them further from this natural world. Mysterious rituals or alarming acts may demand the full attention of those involved, and, hence, usher them corporately into the spiritual realm.

All of this is disgusting and abominable in the sight of God.

Pain also is used by some spiritists as a path to enter the spiritual world. In the inflicting of pain or the experience of pain, there may be the total detachment of one's conscious mind from the natural realm. In the person's attempt to escape from extreme pain, he may reach with all of his strength into the spiritual dimension. Hence, we understand that those involved in sadism, masochism, and other forms of pain inducement find their pleasure not in the pain itself, but in the experience of power or some touch of the spiritual.

The Sun Dance, carried out by some of the native American Indians years ago, included such an entrance into the spiritual world. Hooks were driven through the pectoral muscles of willing men, and then those men were suspended by ropes attached to those hooks. We understand that in the endurance of such pain, many may, indeed, have escaped this natural world and touched spirit beings on the other side.

Sexual intercourse is another means of entrance into the spiritual realm. In the act, those involved completely detach from this world for a moment in time and focus their entire beings upon each other. This focus opens their spirit to bond with their partner. Of course, we would condemn all sexual encounters carried out during the ceremonies of witches and warlocks. However, we do recognize that every sexual encounter, even in marriage, is a spiritual experience.

There are various other means by which people have gone into and experienced the spiritual realm. It is not our intention here to teach them or cover this subject fully. It is the principle that we are most interested in relaying to you. Whenever people focus their entire mind and heart, detaching from the natural world, they may be opening their spirit to the spiritual world. We are not condemning categorically all experiences of the spiritual dimension. Please do not think that. We are warning people that there are certain "illegal avenues of entrance" that will expose people only to the powers of darkness. There are some helps, such as the use of music, which are not to be thought of as evil, but caution should be used, and those involved must keep their hearts directed toward God.

As we conclude this chapter, some readers may be wondering what it is that motivates people to want to experience the spiritual dimension. Many of those who attempt to go into the spirit simply are hoping to escape the pressures and trials of this life. Others are desiring a certain pleasurable feeling. Those trained in evil spiritual practices may be attempting to

seeking of purpose which
sense and meaning it offers.
**How Evil Spiritists Tap into the Spirit Realm**

contact a spirit being or to obtain some spiritual power. However, the vast majority of people who attempt to experience the spiritual world are seeking the sense of *purpose and meaning which it offers.*

Consider that last statement carefully. The spiritual world is the realm in which our inner man is anchored; therefore, to experience that realm is to *get in touch with our roots.* A heart in turmoil can be brought to rest with one glimpse of the spiritual realm. When an individual opens his spirit to encounter that world, he may be overwhelmed by a sense of meaning. In a natural world filled with difficulties, a spiritual experience can restore to an individual a sense of sanity and purpose: indeed, a sense of existence, itself, as being more than merely physical.

Please do not take this wrong. I am not giving credence to false spiritual experiences. Those having encounters apart from the true God can become deceived terribly. What we are trying to explain here is simply the reason so many people hunger for spiritual contact. Of course, there are other reasons, but the desire for meaning is the single most powerful motivating force. The Bible tells us that God has placed eternity in the heart of man (Eccl. 3:11). Every human being, no matter where he or she lives, has a desire for things beyond this natural realm. Spiritual hunger exists in every individual. Therefore, if the Church is not there to guide people into the truth, they will be driven by their hunger toward evil ends.

Let's summarize by saying that both the Christian and the non-Christian tap into the spirit by focusing their souls. Christians and non-Christians encounter

focusing their souls

different aspects of the spiritual world. There is only one spiritual world, but in that world both Satan's kingdom and God's kingdom exist. The spirits of all men also exist in that dimension, along with many other things about which we will learn. Concerning these spiritual realities, every human being has spiritual senses which can perceive that with which his spirit is in contact. The individual may be conscious of his spiritual sensitivities according to the degree that his soul is directed. These are spiritual realities designed in the creation itself and in how God made mankind.

One spiritual world
God's kingdom - satan's kingdom
spirits of all men.

# 5

## How the Human Brain is Affected

It will be enlightening at this point for us to discuss the human "brain" and "mind."

When we talk about the *brain,* we will be referring to the physical organ located in the cranial cavity of each person.  The word *mind* is used in many different ways in different contexts, but here we will use the word *mind* to refer to the invisible part of our being which processes information and governs our thinking processes.

In order to further clarify the distinction between the brain and the mind, we can say that the *brain* is the organ which allows the *mind* contact with the natural world.  The brain also functions to keep the physical body operating properly.  When we die, the brain ceases to function; however, the mind stays conscious in the spirit realm.  The mind is a part of man's invisible side, and the brain is a part of his physical being.

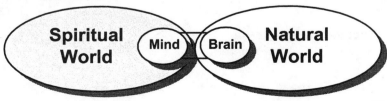

Spiritual World — Mind — Brain — Natural World

# The Spiritual World and How We Access It

The mind and the brain are interwoven in every aspect of their functions. Thought processes in the mind influence the functions of the human brain and vice versa. There is an intimate correspondence between the activities of the two.

Some interesting studies have been done on the functions of the human brain. For example, we know that the left side of the brain is most strongly activated when we are engaged in logical, analytical thinking. The right side of the brain becomes more active whenever people allow creative thought processes to captivate them. Of course, the entire brain always is functioning to some degree, but we simply are noting here increased activity which can be measured.

Associate these scientific observations with what we know about man's makeup. When the mind of a man is directed to the natural realm, along with very active, logical thought, the left side of the brain is most active. When the conscious mind is pointed toward the spirit, the right side of the brain is being used predominantly. The focus of a person's mind influences the functioning of the human brain.

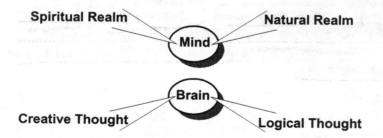

Another equally significant, scientifically observed fact is how the brain waves are affected when people are engaged in different thought processes. When people are relaxed and thinking creatively, what we call *alpha brain waves* flow through the human brain. These can be measured with instruments sensitive to tiny electrical impulses moving through the brain. When people are busy and involved in active, logically oriented work, *beta brain waves* are predominant. These changes between alpha and beta waves are clear physiological changes that can be observed as people alter their thinking patterns.

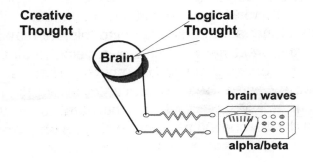

Alpha brain waves are especially strong when people relax and calm themselves. Artistic, inventive types of individuals tend to have more of this type of brain activity. All people have alpha waves predominant when dreaming while asleep. People actually change the flow of electrical impulses from beta to alpha waves as they simplify the thoughts within and focus on one or two basic concepts of their lives.

# The Spiritual World and How We Access It

Those with scientific training in these areas may consider these statements an oversimplification, and, indeed, they are. Within the human brain are many different regions and functions. There are people who have spent years studying the measurable activities of the brain. It is extremely complex and we only have begun to understand how it works. Here we simply are making a few basic observations.

What we do want you to recognize is how certain changes in brain activity can be measured and how these changes correspond with changes in the mind.

For example, when one opens oneself to the realm of the spirit, there is a measurable increase in alpha brain wave activity. As we explained in earlier chapters, one opens to the spirit by detaching from the natural world and focusing his mind. We understand that as a person is doing this, he may be allowing the creativity within his own being to stir, or he may be opening up to the spiritual dimension. Either way, spiritual energy is being released to flow within the individual's mind. At the same time, the physical brain shows an increase in alpha brain waves.

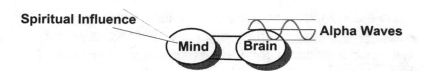

Spiritual Influence — Mind — Brain — Alpha Waves

Do not make the mistake of equating alpha or beta waves with spiritual energy. That would be wrong. We are pointing out a correspondence between the spiritual part of man and the natural.

When a person is tapped into the spirit, the natural brain shows a change in the type of impulses flowing through it.

In order to be healthy, all people require periods of both alpha and beta waves flowing through their brain. People who spend almost all of their time in the creative aspects without a return to normal life, sooner or later find their beings demanding a recovery time. Depression, sleeplessness, emotional extremes, and physical illnesses are all common. Others who spend extended periods with only beta waves predominant, sooner or later, experience a burn-out and need a prolonged rest. These symptoms and others are the result of remaining in a state of mind with only alpha waves or only beta waves being predominant. Being healthy requires living as whole people — the way God created man to live.

As we talk about states of mind, we do not want to limit ourselves to the two extremes involving only alpha or only beta waves. The range from the creative to the logic-controlled side is broad. There are many different conditions in which the mind can function.

Concerning these different states of mind, people involved in various occult groups today use the terminology, "altered states of consciousness" or ASC. Although Christians hesitate to borrow such vocabulary, we should not be threatened by mere words. If we change these mystical sounding terms into ideas which are more familiar to us, perhaps they will not be as scary, and then we can see if there is any validity to the related concepts.

Please let me reassure you that the mystics and the leaders do not have some magical secret buried in this phrase, "altered states of consciousness." The word "altered" simply means "changed," and when we say "altered states of consciousness," that is a phrase referring to the changes in the mind which occur when people change the focus of their attention from one thing to another. It is that simple. Please do not be intimidated by these terms simply because they may be unfamiliar to you.

When Christians examine these concepts from a Biblical perspective, they can see both good and evil in the related teachings. On the positive side, we as Christians recognize altered states of consciousness. We need not deny scientific facts, and, in reality, we experience many different states of mind in our daily lives. Whenever Christians seek God with any degree of seriousness, whether or not they realize it, they are opening themselves to the spiritual realm to such an extent that strong alpha waves are at work; and their state of mind is definitely different (altered) from when they are working in their normal daily activities. The Bible itself teaches us to calm our souls and focus upon the things of the Spirit at specific times of our lives. In many passages of the Bible, people are encouraged to meditate on the things of God. Of course, we are not referring to meditating on evil as non-Christian mystics might do; but thinking deeply on the nature of God and His Word is a vital aspect of the Christian's life. The results of such activities of the mind are no less an altered state than the New Ager meditating on the latest mystical revelation. Our God laid out clear principles for taking time to rest and time to work which both produce altered conditions within our being.> In these ways, the Christian experiences many states of consciousness — simply as he lives his daily life in accordance with God's will.

There are also specific incidents recorded in the Bible that reveal various men and women of God experiencing some of the most radical extremes of altered states of consciousness.

The single most intense experience a human being can have is to encounter God's manifest presence. Make no mistake about this. When Isaiah saw the Lord sitting on His throne (Is. 6:1-7), he was having "a way-out experience." When Paul was taken up to God, he did not know whether he was "in the body or apart from the body" (II Cor. 12:2-4). When the Apostle John beheld Jesus, as recorded in the Book of Revelation, he fell as a dead man (Rev. 1:17). Peter, James, and John had no less of a radical shift in their conscious mind when they saw Jesus in His glory, standing with Moses and Elijah on the Mount of Transfiguration (Matt. 17:1-9). To these, we could add the experiences of Moses seeing God, all the Jews before Mount Sinai, the priests in the Temple as the glory cloud fell, the disciples in the upper room, and all of the early believers as they gathered in the building which began to shake as the Spirit came upon them. W e even read in the Bible about people going into "trances." A trance occurs when the mind becomes so locked onto the spirit that consciousness of the natural world is completely severed. The Apostle Peter, we are told, went into a trance when God spoke to him as he was praying on the rooftop of Simon the tanner's house (Acts 10:9-16). Saul had a similar experience on the road to Damascus (Acts 9:3-8), as did Stephen when he was being stoned to death (Acts 7:55-56). In light of these and other such experiences, it seems quite foolish for any Christian today to deny the reality of altered states of the human mind and brain.

We need to include here the state of mind of people when God talks to them in their sleep. Job 33:14-16, tells us:

> "Indeed God speaks once,
> Or twice, yet no one notices it.
> In a dream, a vision of the night,
> When sound sleep falls on men,
> While they slumber in their beds,
> Then He opens the ears of men,
> And seals their instructions...."

Of course, we realize that not every dream is God's communication with man. In a later volume, we will explain more clearly the function of dreams. Here we simply want to point out that while a person is asleep, he is detached from the natural realm and in an ideal state of mind to receive from God.

Finally, we must mention again the role that visions can play in the life of the Christian. We briefly discussed these in chapter two, but it is worth mentioning again here that a vision is the opening of a person's spiritual eyes to see into the realm of the spirit. By definition, a vision is an altered state of consciousness.

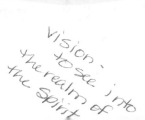

Vision -
to see into
the realm of
the Spirit

Of course, God can communicate with a person without changing the state of his mind. God does use man's logical reasoning, and He expects us to use it to our maximum potential. However, we as whole Christians also must recognize the reality of how God created us. We were created with a wide range of conscious abilities. Almost every time the Bible reveals an instance when God supernaturally communicated with men, those individuals were not in a logic-oriented frame of mind. Think of Jacob as he slept and beheld a ladder extending from heaven to earth with angels ascending and descending upon it (Gen. 28:10-13). Jacob was in a state of mind sensitive to the spiritual realm. In almost every such case in the Bible, the people involved were not in a rationalistic state. They were tapped into the spirit, either by their own attempts to seek God, or by God's act of intervening in their lives.

We need, however, to end this discussion with a warning. Those involved with the occult and various forms of mystical experiences talk much about altered states, and they do, indeed, open themselves to the spiritual realm. If they are not Christians, they will be denied entrance into the kingdom of God, and they expose themselves to demonic deceptions and attacks. Furthermore, the wise Christian does not make it his aim to have an altered state of consciousness. His aim will be to seek God, worship Him, and receive from His nature. As the believer does these things, his state of mind may change. But the goal is to find God, not change the function of one's mind. We, as believers, can understand these

*My aim — seek God*
*worship Him*
*receive His nature*

*tapped in to the spirit Warning — the goal is to find God - not the experience* principles, and, indeed, such understanding may aid us in approaching God. However, our goal is God, not mystical experiences.

## Escaping into the Spirit

Throughout this book we will be stressing the importance of being "whole Christians." We have shown how people can focus either upon the spirit or upon the natural. We explain this not so that Christians will do only one, but that they might understand this two-fold nature of man. We exist in two worlds and are responsible for our activities in both. It is from the spirit that we draw inspiration, purpose, and divine direction. That which we receive then is to be worked out in the natural. This is how God created man.

Some groups of Christians emphasize only one side of their existence: the natural or the spiritual. Either extreme is wrong.

Years ago, I was involved in a church organization that focused only upon the natural, rational side of life. My teachers stressed the importance of education and training. Sound, logical doctrine was valued above everything else. Frequently, the leaders would exhort others, saying, "God gave you a brain, so use it!" By saying this, they were trying to encourage everyone to use the rational side of their brain. Today, years later, I believe that God wants us to use our logic; but by telling people to be solely logic-oriented, we are, in fact, encouraging them to use only a portion of their brain. God created us to be whole people. There are times when one must use all of one's energy to function in everyday life, and there must also be times when a person must focus his attention upon the spiritual things.

Christians with an extreme emphasis on the rational and natural side of life tend to have a difficult time receiving anything from the Spirit. At least, they are not conscious of the Holy Spirit speaking, leading, or revealing anything to them. Why?

Some have been taught wrongly that the spiritual dimension is evil and should be ignored totally by the Christian. Wrong teaching along these lines closes the door to the spiritual dimension. It is faith that allows our spiritual senses to open and our conscious thought to be receptive. Of course, the doubter of these things still is influenced by the spiritual forces acting upon him. He is simply unaware of what is happening. Biblical instruction concerning how the spiritual things function can remove fear and bring an understanding necessary for a godly receptivity.

Other people are unaware of the spiritual dimension simply because they have been trained to keep their conscious thoughts focused upon the natural and logical. Their mind is so programmed to natural ways of thinking and logical thought patterns that spiritual input entering their spirit cannot be received consciously. The concepts of a spiritual nature conflict with those of a structured, reason-based nature. Because of their training, they are detached from the spiritual side of their make-up.

At the other extreme, there are people — Christians and non-Christians — who are more in tune with their spiritual senses than the natural. In some ways, they are detached from the natural world.

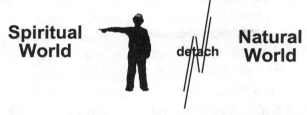

People of this second type, who are intensely in tune with the spirit, often have a difficult time functioning in everyday life. Certain individuals can have their mind so fixed on the spirit and be opened to input only of the spiritual nature that logical thought is difficult for them. Thinking about natural concerns, such as those involving money, family responsibilities, and employment, seems out of reach to them. Their minds will not function along normal lines of thought. Some of the most spiritually sensitive people are so detached from this realm that they are sometimes referred to as "spaced out," "checked out," or "far gone." I like the term, "MEGO," formed from the first letters of the words, "My Eyes Glazed Over!"

## The Spiritual World and How We Access It

How do such people get that way? Some become fixated upon the spiritual dimension through repeated choices to focus only there. Many people escape this world (at least consciously), by retreating into their own imaginations. Such creative thought tends to draw on the spiritual side. Some steer their lives in that direction because circumstances around them are very stressful. Children who grow up in abusive homes, or where they suffer much rejection, have a tendency to deal with the pressure by detaching. The stimulus for others to seek refuge in the spirit may be trials, such as long-term financial lack, marital turmoil, or physical pain. Others, for no set reason, but just by choice, spend hours day-dreaming, feeling sorry for themselves, fantasizing, or drawing on inspirations from the spiritual side.

There are also people who have a tendency to focus upon the spirit from birth. Among these are those with very artistic, inventive, or creative personalities. A few seem to inherit spiritual recep-tivity. This can originate from either a godly parent or one tapped into evil demonic powers. Witches sometime are known to pass their spiritual abilities to their children and grandchildren. In similar fashion, openness of spirit can be passed on from one committed to God. Later, we will separate an evil receptivity from a good receptivity. For now, however, let us recognize that some people are especially opened to the spirit as a result of gifts they already have from birth, which may be inherited abilities from others.

There are many others who have a hard time functioning in the natural world because they have damaged their brains and souls through the use of drugs. Both alcohol and drugs can be used to numb the conscious mind. It is for this reason that many people use one or the other to block out, and hence, temporarily escape their natural responsibilities. Through repeated use, the individual becomes more and more detached from the natural world, as far as his conscious thought is concerned.

There are also people who fixate on the spiritual side because of their belief system. Eastern religious thought, in particular, promotes this lifestyle. For example, the Buddhist religion teaches its followers to pursue "nirvana" through meditation and various exercises. "Nirvana" is thought to be a condition of "total bliss" or "oneness with the cosmos." In reality, it is simply the condition in which a person is completely detached from natural responsibilities and wide open to the world of the spirit. This philosophy of life also is promoted by many New Age teachers.

Tragically, this deception has crept into some Christian circles today. Even though they do not use Buddhist terminology, they stress the spiritual side to the exclusion of the natural. They start thinking and believing that God wants them to live every day and every minute with their mind entirely focused upon the spiritual dimension.

You must see this as a wrong concept of what the Christian life actually is. Paul prayed that we may be sanctified entirely, body, soul, and spirit (I Thess. 5:23). God never intended us to deny or reject a part of our nature. The message of the Gospel is redemption. That redemption is for our entire being. God desires for us to use our mind, emotions, and all of our strength in serving Him.

Some Christians, misunderstanding this, have tried to structure their life by only doing what they perceive from the spirit. They attempt to make all their decisions only on the basis of visions, dreams, spiritual stirrings, revelations, etc. As they attempt to live this way, they deny what their natural bodies and their logical minds are dictating to them.

Initially, such a lifestyle may sound very holy and right to some people. But, in fact, it is wrong.

God's intention is *that we live our lives in touch with both the natural and spiritual world.* The mind of a man must be conscious of both. There will be occasions when a Christian should set aside time to detach from the natural world in order to seek God with all of his heart and soul. But for most of our daily lives, we are called to function in this world. For example, when hunger is felt in the physical body, it usually should be fed. If a Christian gets a flat tire on his car, he can use his head to get out and fix it, without waiting for second-by-second instructions from the Holy Spirit. God designed us with the mechanism to live here successfully. And that means being able to interact with this natural realm, evaluate the information we receive, and make decisions with our own free will. Of course, the Christian should be open anytime to receive input from the spirit, but that is not to be his sole conscious focus of attention. He was created to be a whole man, in touch with both the natural and the spiritual world.

To see this in the Bible, look at John's words in Revelation 1:10. There John tells us, "I was in the Spirit on the Lord's day,...." He went on to explain all that he received concerning visions, revelations, prophetic messages, and future events. Even though John's spiritual senses were opened in this way for a time, he did not remain in that condition. By saying he was in the spirit "on the Lord's day," he implied that he was not in it every day or constantly. The state of being completely conscious of that dimension was temporary.

The men and women in the Book of Acts lived similarly. We read about leaders like Paul and Peter sometime receiving visions and dreams, but at other times making very naturally-based decisions. For example, throughout the fifteenth chapter of Acts, we see the early Church leaders discussing, debating, and using their minds to make decisions about key issues for their time. Of course, we believe that the Holy Spirit was guiding them, but it is important to note that they used more than spiritual input to govern their lives.

Some Christians would point to Jesus and try to tell us that He made all of His decisions on the sole basis of the guidance He received through His spirit. He did tell us that He did nothing on His own initiative, and that He only did what the Father showed Him (John 5:19, 30). However, this does not mean that He walked around with a glazed-over look in His eyes. On the contrary, Jesus was fully human, yet divine. He had a pure, untainted mind. His soul was holy. His body was not corrupted by sin. Therefore, for Him to do what seemed natural to Him would have been always, in every circumstance, the will of the Father. His motivations were perfect, and therefore, the decisions He made by His free will always would have been in perfect agreement with the Father. In saying that He only did what the Father showed Him, He was not telling us that He walked around in a semi-conscious state. God just as easily could have shown Him things through His perfectly sanctified mind and even through His natural senses. The Father led the Son through His entire being.

More will be said about successful Christian living in Volume III, but please understand here that the Christian is not to live with his mind fixed toward the spirit. In pointing this out, we are not saying that the human mind should have the authority position in a believer's life; nor should a person be ruled by his natural desires or emotions. We are not giving credence to any of those lifestyles. We simply are stating at this point that the Christian should endeavor to live as a *wholly* sanctified person.

We are addressing this issue here because we do not want our readers to misunderstand how the fullness of the Christian life is to be lived. We will be continuing in this book to teach primarily upon the spiritual dimension, but please do not let that become the sole focus in your life. Perhaps I am concerned more intensely about this issue because I know that the type of Christians most interested in reading a book such as this one are the very ones with a strong drawing to the spiritual dimension.

There are numerous problems we see developing in the lives of Christians who are solely spirit-oriented. For example, it is common for deceptions to enter into their thought patterns. When the mind is not grounded in the natural and logical realm, it may begin to "float and drift on the waves of spiritual energy." As a boat that is not anchored, so is the mind that is not in touch with natural reality. Such a person's patterns of thought may become perverted. Frequently, we see them developing bizarre ideas and ways of thinking. Christians in this trap often come up with weird doctrines, fully convinced they are of God. The longer a person remains fixated only upon the spirit, the further he can be pulled off the path of reality and truth.

In addition to the above problems, excessively spirit-oriented people tend to develop various sexual and emotional problems. Because they detach from things of this world, they may cut themselves off emotionally or entirely from normal relationships. As a consequence, their own needs may go unmet. They may try to deny those needs for a time, but sooner or later their unfulfilled needs will rise and take control (unless God has given them a special gift to deal with these problems as mentioned in Matthew 19:11). After God created Adam, He said that it was not good for a man to be alone (Gen. 2:18). The person who repeatedly detaches will have voids in his makeup that demand satisfaction. Bizarre behaviors and unnatural desires often develop. Some of the most spirit-focused Christians eventually develop compulsive actions, sexually perverted thoughts, unnatural views of the marriage relationship, uncontrolled fantasizing, overeating tendencies, homosexual desires, groundless fears, loneliness, and suicidal tendencies.

Because these Christians try to explain everything in terms of spiritual realities, they remain blind as to how to get free. If someone offers them

**65**

the only real solution, *that they have to change their lifestyle and get more naturally oriented*, they tend to reject the advice as evil and contrary to the leading of God in their life. They would rather put all their energy into rebuking the devil, fasting, and going deeper into the spirit. Typically, they experience temporary relief through such endeavors, but over the long run, their problems only are amplified. Some will listen only after months or years of seeing that "their way of living" does not work. It does not produce the victorious Christian life which they have been seeking.

The Bible has much to say about the benefits of good, hard, honest work. It is healing. So also proper relationships must be maintained if a Christian is to remain emotionally sound. The Apostle Paul wrote to the early believers not to separate from their spouses for prayer for too long of a period, lest Satan come and find opportunity in their lives (I Cor. 7:5). This warning is just as critical for today's Christians. Detachment is to be temporary for the purpose of seeking God. The overcoming Christian life is one of functioning and producing in very real natural ways and maintaining healthy relationships in marriage and with other believers.

There have been some severe cases of fixation upon the spirit, where people are unable to bring their conscious mind back to natural reality. We consider such people mentally insane. Some of them become so directed spiritually that demonic activity becomes involved.

I have found that the best way to help people who have become fixated on the spirit is to "make"

*[handwritten margin note: Proper relationships must be maintained]*

them redirect their conscious mind. If demonic activity is involved, a believer who understands his authority should command the devil to leave in Jesus' name. After that, the individual must redirect his mind actively and aggressively. The best way to treat a person detached from the natural is to "make" him do something natural. The best therapy for an ex-drug user may be an eight-to-five manual labor job. For some Christian who has been a dreamer all his life, you may have to speak to him very authoritatively and help him actually think about his financial situation. The one who is neglecting his family should be sternly corrected. All may need to be taught that the lifestyle solely directed toward the spirit is Biblically wrong. Sometime this transition is very hard for the individual — but it is essential.

Let me qualify all that by saying that we do not want to close the doors to the spiritual realm. Every Christian should have times during which he focuses his entire being toward God. Some people are more prophetically or spiritually inclined by God's design, and we do not want to quench the Holy Spirit in them, nor do we want to destroy the creativity of the artist or musician. In no way do we want to condemn or reject those who have special giftings in these areas. We merely hope to teach how the whole man is to function and to help people live, fulfilling their maximum potential in God.

That is accomplished when a Christian lives his or her life in touch with both the spiritual and the natural world. Anyone who uses the spirit as an escape from natural responsibilities is wrong. They may be seriously earnest in their pursuit of God, but they are deceived if they think God is pleased with their lifestyle. The spirit world is not an escape route. It is the realm from which we receive inspiration, purpose, and direction, but that which is received in the spirit must be worked out in the natural. To bring forth that which is received in the spirit requires a sound mind, logical thinking, discipline, and a healthy body.

# 7

## Doorways to the Spiritual World

To this point, we have discussed much concerning our contact and interaction with the spiritual world. Now we can add to our understanding another major point, which is: how people can function as *doorways* for the spiritual world to enter and influence the natural world. As a passageway between two rooms, so also every human being stands at the threshold between the two worlds. In that position, we each possess the ability to release spiritual things into the natural realm. Let me explain how this functions.

*people fm as doorways*

**Spiritual World**

**Natural World**

When God created the world, He spoke over mankind and gave him dominion over the earth (Gen. 1:28). With that declaration, God imparted to mankind authority over this earth. This truth is revealed in other Scripture passages, as well. For example, Psalm 115:16 tells us:

> The heavens are the heavens
> of the Lord;
> But the earth He has given to
> the sons of men.

God has delegated to us the authority over this earth. Since we have this authority, we decide what influences — good or evil — come into this world.

In reference to evil, we first can give the example of Adam. We are told in the Bible that because of Adam's sin, death entered the world:

> ...through one man sin entered
> into the world, and death
> through sin, and so death
> spread to all men, because all
> sinned... (Rom 5:12).

Notice the entrance point for sin and death: a human being. Once sin and death had entered the world, it spread to all mankind. Adam was the first doorway.

< Every human being serves as a doorway to some degree.> Every time we yield to the temptations of the devil, we are giving him access to work through us and, hence, influence this world. Every time we obey God, we are giving Him access to this realm. Of course, God is sovereign and He does not need man's permission before acting in our world; however, to some degree He does limit His intervention in the affairs of men and chooses to work through yielded vessels.

We can see specific means by which spiritual entities move from the spiritual world into the natural realm. In understanding this phenomena, we use the term *manifestation*. For example, if an angel were sitting next to you right now, you could not see it nor touch it. That angel would be invisible to you, even though it were present. However, if that angel *manifested*, it would come out of its world and reveal itself to you so that you could see it, touch it, or in some way sense its presence. It is in this context that we talk about spiritual entities *manifesting*.

## Spiritual World          Natural World

Not only do angels and demons manifest, but God Himself often does. God does not have a physical body, although He could manifest in any form that He desired. We can read in the Bible how He manifested in the forms of fire, wind, a cloud, shining light, etc. God also has manifested in the earth through His Son, Jesus (John 14:9; Heb. 1:3).

The Holy Spirit of God manifests in this world, and what is most interesting in our discussion here is how He manifests through Christians in the form of gifts which He gives. The Apostle Paul explained:

> But to each one is given the manifestation of the Spirit for the common good (I Cor. 12:7).

*Holy Spirit manifests through us*

71

After this verse, Paul listed the nine spiritual gifts, the avenues by which the Holy Spirit comes into this world. When the Holy Spirit gives gifts of tongues, prophecy, and interpretation of tongues, He speaks through a believer, so that listeners can hear Him. When there are gifts of healings and miracles or faith manifesting, it is the Holy Spirit coming out of His world and into this world to demonstrate His power, love, and will. When a Christian receives from the Holy Spirit words of knowledge, words of wisdom, or the gift of discerning of spirits, it is the Holy Spirit revealing to the person the thoughts of God. Each of these nine gifts is a way in which the Holy Spirit comes out of His world and into this natural realm.

**Holy Spirit Manifestations:**

**Prophecy**
**Tongues & Interpretation**
**Miracles & Healing**
**Faith**
**Words of Wisdom**
**Words of Knowledge**
**Distinguishing of Spirits**

There are many other ways in which spiritual realities, both good and bad, move from the spiritual world into the natural world. We will discuss them further as we continue, but here our main objective is to help you see that human beings can act as doorways between the two worlds.

In reference to this, God has given specific authority to Christians. Jesus said to His disciples:

"I will give you the keys of the kingdom of heaven; and whatever you shall bind on earth shall be bound in heaven, and whatever you shall loose on earth shall be loosed in heaven" (Matt. 16:19).

This God-given authority includes the ability to influence the spiritual world from the natural world and to bring certain spiritual influences into the natural world.

We will be teaching throughout this book that this authority was not given only to the early disciples, but extends to all Christians, even today.

However, do not jump to the false conclusion that we can use this authority whenever or however we choose. The Apostle Paul taught us that the kingdom of God consists of "righteousness and peace and joy *in the Holy Spirit*" (Rom. 14:17). The important point is that this authority is granted to us as we yield to the leading of the Holy Spirit in our daily lives. Some Christians have missed this vital truth and attempted to manifest God's power apart from being submitted to Him. We will be teaching that Christians do have authority to bind or loose the kingdom of God, but only to the extent that they are being led by the Holy Spirit of God.

Now, we need to include in our understanding the role which non-Christians can play as doorways for spiritual things to come into the natural world. It is a fact that there are evil witches who are submitting their lives to certain demonic powers and, hence, bringing the related powers into this natural world. New Age practitioners do draw upon spiritual energies. Peoples of many different cultures tap into various evil forces. They are, indeed, acting as doorways. Yes, evil people do have authority to bring the spiritual world into the natural world. When God spoke that man will have dominion over this earth, He imparted the related authority. Even evil people, therefore, have the power to bind or loose.

The important distinction between the Christian and the non-Christian is that we have the power to bind or loose *the kingdom of God*. Non-Christians can go into the spiritual world and bind or loose certain powers there, but unless a man is born again, he cannot see or enter the kingdom of God (John 3:3-5). Therefore, when a non-Christian goes into the spiritual world and uses its power, he or she is forbidden access to God, the blessings of God, or the kingdom of God. Yes, evil people can exercise spiritual power, but no, that power is not from the kingdom of light.

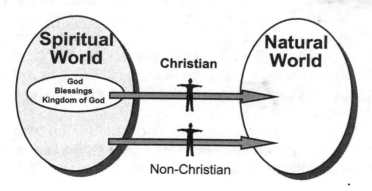

Finally, let's add to our understanding the fact that there are certain *keys* to releasing the spiritual realm into the natural. For many people, the spiritual realm seems like a distant world which cannot be tapped — the door seems to be sealed. However, Jesus told us that He has given us the *keys to the kingdom.* Think of the keys that open the door to your house or that start your car. Keys are very small items which unlock great power and give us access to previously closed areas. What then are these keys which we have been given? In the next two chapters we will see.

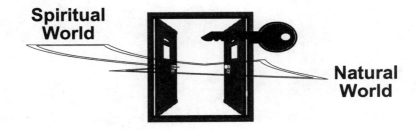

**Spiritual World**

**Natural World**

# Keys that Open the Door to the Spirit Realm

The doorway between the spiritual world and the natural world can be opened by any person. God has given man authority over this natural realm and, therefore, over what comes into this world. However, as we learned in the last chapter, only the Christian has access to the kingdom of God and His blessings.

How things are released from one world into the other is very similar to how people *tune in to the spirit*. We explained in chapters three and four, how people can detach from the natural world, focus their attention, and hence, open themselves to the spiritual realm. In that condition, they are open not only to receive information but also to release the spiritual realm into the natural, whether good or bad.

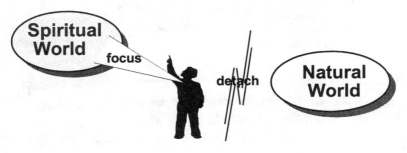

To see this, consider our Lord's words in Matthew 6:22-24:

> "The lamp of the body is the eye; if therefore your eye is clear, your whole body will be full of light. But if your eye is bad, your whole body will be full of darkness. If therefore the light that is in you is darkness, how great is the darkness!"

First of all notice from our Lord's words here, the nature of the light or darkness which fills a person. This is not referring to a natural light bulb illuminating a person's internal organs. These words are spiritual references. Spiritual light or spiritual darkness fills a person, depending upon the focus of his eye.

Next, examine the eye about which our Lord is teaching. He is not speaking of the two physical organs which give natural vision. He is talking about the entire perspective of a person's life: the orientation of his affections, desires, and faith. In the verse preceding the one we just quoted, Jesus said:

> "for where your treasure is, there will your heart be also." (Matt 6:21).

Notice in this context the association Jesus was making between singleness of eye and the direction in which a person's heart is pointed. We know from other Bible verses that the heart is the seat of faith, love, and desires (i.e., Rom. 10:10; Luke 24:32; II Peter 2:14). Proverbs 4:23 tells us that from the heart flows all the issues of life. As recorded in Ephesians 1:18, the Apostle Paul prayed that the eyes of the Christian's heart would be enlightened. The eye, in this sense, refers to the basic orientation of a person's heart; hence, upon what he believes and focuses his life.

I hesitate even to use the word *focus*, because too many people associate this term with a *fixed mindset*. We are not talking about clinging to a certain set of thoughts in one's mind. Nor are we telling people to take on an intense, forceful frame of mind. It is the *heart* to which we are referring here. The characteristic of heart of which we are speaking, has to do with a *specific orientation*. The proper orientation does not require an intense, serious demeanor. A person with singleness of eye may be joyful, relaxed, and at peace. In fact, a person with the right heart may be laughing and having a great time. Emotions can come and go. Thought patterns may change. But a person who is single of eye has the orientation of his heart in one direction.

In Matthew 6, where Jesus taught us to have our eye single, He went on to say:

> "No one can serve two masters" (Matt 6:24).

The truth we learn here is that upon whatever people set their hearts, they actually bow and serve as their master.

What then will happen to a person whose eye is single?  Depending upon what he is focused, he will be filled with spiritual light or darkness.  This light and darkness within a person does not remain confined to the limits of his physical body.  Jesus explained that whatever enters the heart of a person flows out of his mouth and influences his entire life (Matt. 15:18-19; 12:33-35).  So then, a person whose eye is single, releases spiritual power throughout all the various aspects of his life.

**Single of eye**

The proper focus for the Christian is, of course, toward God.  We must understand that this involves more than going to church or having an occasional thought about Him.  Rather, it is yielding to a loving, powerful, giving, concerned Father.

To verify this, read the context of Matthew 6. There Jesus gave specific instructions concerning where our eye should be set.  He told the disciples to look at the birds of the air and the lilies of the field (Matt. 6:26-28).  He went on to explain how God provides for all these, and that certainly He will take care of us.  The point, then, is not simply for us to look at birds or lilies, but at a God who is good, powerful, and loving toward us.  In contrast, Jesus also talked

*good powerful loving*

about the person who has his eye set upon his own needs and lack. The one whose heart is anxious, worried, and/or greedy actually is bowing to mammon, rather than focusing upon the goodness of God. He whose heart is at peace, knowing that God will provide, has the eye of his heart set in the proper place (Is. 26:3).

Two different results we may see. He whose eye is set on God and His goodness will have all things added unto him (Matt. 6:33). He whose eye is set on problems, needs, and lack (or has a concept of God being evil, harsh, or cruel), will have a curse released over his own life.

God and His goodness

All things added

Blessings

This focus of one's eye is the most important key to releasing spiritual power into this world.

Some of my readers may be disappointed at this point. In the last chapter and this one, I have been building you up to discover keys that unlock tremendous power and spiritual blessings. Now, I am telling you basically that the focus of one's attention simply being on God and His goodness is a key which will accomplish this very thing. Perhaps you were wanting to hear some hidden mystery that no other person knows. Maybe you wanted to read a secret method that will give you more power than witches and New Age practitioners. Well, do not be disappointed, because that is exactly what we have been discussing.

Although it is no secret, the key of focusing one's life on God and His goodness will unlock tremendous powers. In fact, I dare say that a lifestyle in which a  Christian simply keeps his heart directed toward God will open up a spiritual window from which consistent power will flow, greater than any New Ager or the most advanced warlock ever has discovered. Please hear this.

Of course, there are specific methods and techniques which people use to help them release spiritual things into the natural realm. Witches and those in occult practices can tap into spiritual arenas for a momentary burst of spiritual activity. We will discuss some of these in more detail as we continue. We also will see specific means by which Christians can tap into God's blessings. However, before we continue, we must see the bigger picture: a whole lifestyle with one's faith set on God and His goodness will keep the consistent blessings of God flowing and the light within a person shining brightly. This most important spiritual benefit evil men and women cannot possess.

Now let's apply the principle of the focused eye to specific areas.

Allow me to tell you about a tragic incident in which a certain woman died of cancer. This woman, whom I will call Sally, was working as a secretary for a businessman I know. It was not until later in life that Sally married. Right after their wedding, her husband expressed great concern when he discovered a lump on her breast. She explained that the lump had been there for many years and that it was nothing to worry about. However, because of his insistence, she went and had it checked out by a qualified doctor. When the news came back that the lump was cancerous, it consumed both of their thoughts. The cancer spread rapidly and approximately two months later, Sally died.

Cases such as this are not infrequent. A person may have a certain condition for years which seems dormant, or at least insignificant, but then as soon as a person's eyes become fixed upon it, that very evil becomes activated. Now, we are not stating or implying that all cancer or sickness is the result of people's wrong focus. Please do not conclude that. What we are saying is that in some cases, with some illnesses, the related problems seem to have been given power by the focus of the individual.

Everyone has experienced this to some degree. For a common example, consider the person who feels nauseated from motion sickness or a common flu. If they focus on the sickening feeling, they can yield to it quickly and become overtaken by its influence. On the other hand, if they force themselves to think only about the work set before them, they often can overcome the weakness or illness.

In pointing out these examples of physical illness, do not conclude that all sickness is just spiritual in nature. We do know that some diseases involve the activity of demons. The Bible gives us examples of Jesus casting "spirits of infirmity" out of people; and as a consequence, those people were physically healed (i.e. Luke 13:11; Matt. 8:16-17). However, most diseases and illnesses have actual, physical activities involving bacteria, viruses, and/or physical disorders. They have a physical basis which should be treated with the best possible medical help available. We will discuss healing more in Volume II. Here, we simply are acknowledging that some illnesses are spiritual in origin.

Whether we are dealing with physically or spiritually based illness, all people can be strengthened by having the proper focus of their heart. A person whose eye is clear will have greater spiritual strength within himself, resulting in better physical health. A person whose eye is bad will be weakened spiritually, and more likely will be subjected to physical ailments.

Our main point here has to do with the focus of a person's eye and how it opens the door for light and darkness. We can relate this truth to everyday temptations which come into a person's life. For example, if the devil puts an evil thought into an individual's mind, that person will make a decision whether or not to listen. If that evil thought is in line with a person's own lusts and evil desires, he will have a tendency to *tune in* and even *yield his attention to it*. Once that person's eye is focused upon the temptation, he releases its spiritual power into his own life.

temptation

focus

sin

See this principle in action as a fellow, whom we will call Dave, focuses upon all his past failures and the negative attributes of his life. As Dave dwells upon these things, his spiritual strength is drained away. Dave then starts believing he is a failure and helpless. Soon Dave is in depression and is overcome by the circumstances around him.

Now, let's turn our attention to some of the positive workings of this principle. First, we can mention the role of laying hands upon people and praying for them. Consider Judy, who goes to church where the leaders believe in praying for the sick. Judy has been battling with cancer for several months. When she has the church elders pray for her, the focus of her life changes from off the sickness and onto God. As the elders pray, they lay their hands upon her forehead and she yields to the authority and love expressed. Faith rises in her heart, and for the first time she has hope that perhaps she will live through this trial. That time of prayer serves as a *point of contact* for her faith. Wherever she is, at home, driving her car, or even in the doctor's office, she thinks back to the moment when the elders laid hands upon her and prayed. Because she changes her focus, spiritual light within her physical body increases, and she is stronger in fighting the disease. Most important, she has opened the doorway to God so His healing power will flow into her.

Words spoken by a person of authority also can be points of focus for another's heart. For example, many churches believe in prophecy, the gift through which Christians speak out that which is stirring in their spirits by the Holy Spirit. As a believer speaks out, others are listening. Some of the listeners may fix their attention upon a certain message and continue to recall it in their minds again and again. It is in this fashion that prophecy and other words can become keys which open the door to the spiritual realm.

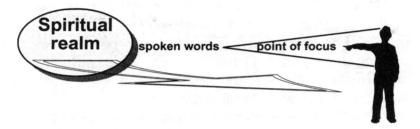

The giving of money often serves as another focal point for one's faith — especially when a person has had to sacrifice in order to give. In Old Testament times, people often would bring an offering to a prophet, which would release the prophet to hear God and give instructions. For example, as Saul and his servant once went to seek counsel from the Prophet Samuel, the servant said:

> "Behold, I have in my hand a fourth of a shekel of silver; I will give it to the man of God and he will tell us our way." (I Samuel 9:8).

Even today, many people have experienced this truth in operation. After giving, even when they themselves are in need, they feel faith (light) rise in their heart, and soon they have the answers they need to overcome the problems they face.

Many other things can serve as points of focus. Some Christians have learned to latch onto the promises of God which are recorded in the Bible, in such a manner that God's power is released. Others have had the orientation of their heart changed at an anointed meeting, while watching a miracle, during an ordination service, after being exposed to the needs of hurting people in third-world countries, etc. Any such events can fixate a person's attention and act as a key to open the spiritual realm.

On the negative side, we also see shaking events captivating a person's heart, such as the death of a loved one, a car wreck, a harsh rebuke, a humiliating experience, the betrayal of a friend, etc. A specific example we can mention is of the war veteran who experienced overwhelming trials on the battlefront. In that condition his eye may have fixed, the orientation of his heart changed, and his spirit opened to the "spirit of war." As a consequence, years later he still may have "flashbacks" of the tragedies he witnessed. These images can be so consuming and possessing that the vet is unable to function in the normal affairs of life. Only after he re-orients his heart, and no longer desires the "spirit of war," will he close his spirit to those related evils, and hence, be free.

In conclusion, we can say that the fixed orientation of a person's heart can open the world of the spirit, both its blessings and curses.

Before we close this chapter, let me add an interesting observation which carries with it a warning. As we explained in an earlier chapter, some people seem to be very sensitive to spiritual things. What they have learned to do is orient their heart toward the spiritual things, and hence, receive spiritual information. *However, the door to listen is the same door as the door to receive.* Therefore, people who are sensitive to the spiritual realm are commonly more subject to its influences than other people.

For example, if two people go into a location of strong demonic activity, one person may immediately feel uneasy and be aware of evil entities. The other more naturally-oriented person may have no such sensations or awareness. What we often see is that the person who is sensitive is also more likely to experience spiritual attacks. He or she may battle with negative thoughts, become physically ill, or have other problems for days after such an exposure. At the same time the naturally-oriented person is not influenced in any noticeable way.

The reason we point this out is for warning purposes. Some people think they simply are receiving spiritual information, when in actuality they are coming under its influence. Also, people who are spiritually sensitive need to be more careful concerning to what they open themselves. Often the door of demonic influence only can be closed when a person hardens himself. Like the war veteran who must choose not to point his heart toward the past or the spirit of war, so also the spiritually sensitive person may have to make himself less sensitive by *refusing to* receive any related spiritual information.

Finally, some Christians have majored their lives in trying to discern devils and fight their influences; but as a consequence, they often suffer the associated attacks. There are some believers whom God has called to minister much in these areas, and we are grateful for their ministries. However, the aim of every Christian's heart must be toward God rather than the pursuit of demons. As a person's focus of life is toward seeking God, the kingdom of darkness is subdued automatically. This, then, must be the focus of the Christian's life.

As a person's focus of life is toward seeking God, the kingdom of darkness is subdued automatically. This must be the focus of the Christians life

## 9

## Incorporating Spiritual Substance

We have been talking about things moving from the spiritual world into the natural. We want you to realize that these "things" have actual literal substance to them. Spiritual things are not made of material like wood or metal, but they do, indeed, exist, and hence, have form, consisting of spiritual substance.

For example, when the Bible tells us that God gives us His Spirit, and that we are "partakers of the divine nature" (II Peter 1:4), we must realize that invisible substance from His own being actually has entered into us.

Furthermore, when the Bible tells us that "God is love" (I John 4:8), we can conclude that this love has actual substance to it. We are told that God has planted His love within our hearts. This is not just a figure of speech, but something actually and literally has been taken from His nature and deposited in our being.

**Spiritual substance**

(In Volume IV we will learn how spiritual substance is transmitted between people, through several avenues, including love.)

Grace, too, has substance. When God gives us grace, He is not giving us just His smile or His good thoughts. No. Literal substance from His nature is released into us. When we think of the spiritual world, we must realize that love, grace, power, and other elements have real substance.

Now, consider how we can transmit spiritual substance from the spiritual world into this natural world through hope and faith. Hebrews 11:1 tells us:

> Now faith is the substance of
> things hoped for, the evidence
> of things not seen (Heb. 11:1
> KJV).

Take this verse literally. Notice the difference between hope and faith. First comes hope, then comes faith. Hope refers to things desired, but not yet received. Faith talks about actually receiving what was earlier hoped for. We are told in this verse that when a person believes, they actually are *receiving the substance* of that for which they were hoping.

Envision this verse in action in the life of Bill, a Christian who is praying for God to heal him. The first time Bill prays he does not really have faith, but he is *hoping* God will answer him. As he prays with hope in his heart, he is reaching out to God in the spirit. It is as if he were "reaching to touch the hem of God's garment," just as the woman in Luke 8:43-48 pressed through the crowd in order to receive our Lord's healing touch. But then after praying, Bill's hope may turn into faith. That moment is when peace enters his heart. But it is not just peace that comes. *Faith is the substance* of that for which he was hoping. Actual, literal substance comes out of the spirit realm and enters into his heart. It is planted there like a seed. The seed which Bill has received in this case, consists of the Word of God, as Bill hears and believes.

**Substance of God's Word**

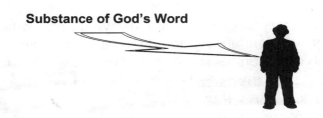

What we need to realize is that everything God has spoken actually has substance, and as we believe Him, we are receiving that substance in our heart. We, therefore, can be a doorway for spiritual things to come into this world, through praying and believing.

We are not presenting this as a formula which people can mechanistically or magically apply. No. God is a person Who is vitally active and concerned about our lives. It is when we come into agreement with His thoughts and desires that His blessings flow into us. Often the doorway is not open apart from His revealing Himself to the person, or in some way having relationship with him. This is relational, not mechanical.

## The Spiritual World and How We Access It

Once we have received the substance of God's Word, it grows in our heart like a seed. Jesus taught us this in many different Bible passages (i.e., Matt. 13:3-23;31-33). The substance of God's Word enters our heart, and then it gradually grows until it comes forth changing our desires and thoughts, and eventually the world around us.

When we teach about prayer, we do not want to limit our understanding to the avenue of entrance through a person. Yes, hope and faith allow spiritual things to pass from one world into another, but God is not limited to working through people. He can act sovereignly whenever He chooses. Furthermore, He answers prayer at times without passing the related substance through an individual. Sometime people pray, and God simply reaches out from His world and intervenes in the affairs of men, according to the prayers He hears. Please keep this in mind as we continue.

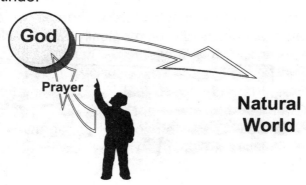

⟨Our interest here is in <u>how people can and do</u> <u>serve as doorways through prayer, as hope turns into</u> <u>faith</u>. Understand at this point that <u>hope is the</u> <u>reaching of a person's spirit into the world of the</u> <u>spirit, and faith is the receiving of the related</u> <u>substance</u>.

Next, let's explain why some spiritual things are harder to obtain than others. That is, the strength of faith required to receive some things must be greater, at times, than the strength of faith to receive other things. God answers our prayers every time we pray according to His will, but there is resistance in the spiritual dimension that actually prohibits our receiving some of His promises. Sometime this is sensed by Christians in prayer as a distance between them and God. It may feel as if "the heavens are brass." Great faith and persistence are required in such cases for the individual to "break through" to God's answer.

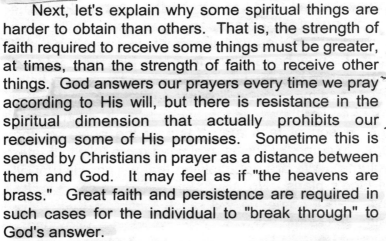

For example, in Daniel 10 we read how Daniel prayed and fasted for twenty-one days before he received the answer to his prayer. An angel then appeared to Daniel bringing God's answer. That angel told Daniel that he had been sent at the time of the first request, but the "Prince of the kingdom of Persia" withstood him and kept him from actually arriving with God's answer. It is in this fashion that God makes His blessings readily available, <u>but</u> men often are required to exercise great faith to overcome certain hindrances in the spiritual realm.

<u>Resistance</u> to our receiving can be caused by several things. Sometime <u>devils</u> will fight to hold God's power, anointings, and will from people's lives.

It is because of this war that Jesus exhorted His followers to keep seeking and asking (Luke 11:1-10). If we continue with persistence, evil resisting forces eventually will give up (James 4:7).

Some things in the spiritual world are difficult to receive because God has not released them at the present time. God has established clear order to the unfolding of His plans and purposes. When an individual reaches into the spirit, through hope and faith, he may be reaching for some blessing that God ordained to be released farther down the road in time. Faith, at times, can pull things and events into fulfillment earlier than God's set schedule. In such cases, the person of faith may "taste of the power of the ages to come." (This is explained more fully in a later volume). We are not implying that we can disrupt all of God's plans. No. But some aspects seem to be available if someone will reach to obtain them. By faith, believers may receive revelations, anointings, and various answers to prayer through such a "drawing in."

There are also spiritual things which cannot be given to an individual without many other elements in the spiritual world being aligned accordingly. For example, a Christian named Mary may be praying to God for an anointing to influence the children in her ministry. As Mary prays, she is drawing on the nature of God. Each time she asks for the anointing, God may be reaching down from heaven and touching the hearts of the children, preparing them to respond to the anointing for which Mary is asking. Then, the very moment Mary receives that anointing in her heart, the children also have had their hearts turned, so that they will be ready to receive ministry from Mary.

What we need to realize here is that nothing exists in the spiritual realm independently. When we ask God for some particular blessing, He may be changing the hearts of people, circumstances, events, and many other related things. Every time some aspect of the spiritual world is obtained by faith, other dimensions of the spiritual kingdoms are bound or loosed. Therefore, to pull within oneself something from the spiritual world often entails tremendous faith.

There also may be required changes within the individual. James 4:3 tells us that sometime we do not receive the answers to our prayers because our own hearts are wrong. Often it is our own heart attitudes which make us unfit to receive the answer. For example, a man may be praying to God for an anointing to reach his nation with the gospel, while at the same time he is consumed with his business and financial concerns. If his entire being is directed in a way contrary to the prayers coming out of his mouth, he will be an unfit vessel to receive. Many characteristics in the individual, such as holiness, a willingness to pay the necessary price, the right heart motivation, etc., can determine whether or not spiritual substance for that which is desired will actually enter the person. In reality, only contact with God and a relationship with Him can prepare an individual to receive that for which he has prayed.

Finally, in discussing why some things seem difficult to draw out of the spiritual realm, we need to simply say, "We don't know." This is a difficult truth for some people to accept because they want everything to fit into nice neat packages. But the truth is that we do not know everything about the spiritual realm and, even more important, God is sovereign. This is an important truth to keep in mind throughout these writings. We do not know everything. What we do know, we teach.

Even though we do not have complete understanding, we do have assurance in our endeavors of pursuing God. Jesus said:

> "Ask, and it shall be given to you; seek, and you shall find; knock, and it shall be opened to you" (Matt. 7:7).

The context of this verse is emphasizing the importance of persistence in our prayers. As people direct their hearts toward God, it is as if their spirit were "reaching to touch the hem of His garment." As they keep longing, hoping, and desiring, they are applying pressure in the spiritual world, which eventually parts the heavens.

Before leaving this subject, let's make a comparison between how we access good things and how we access evil things in the spiritual world.

As we have learned, hope and faith are the avenues through which we draw in God's blessings from the spiritual world. Our focus has been upon the heart of man, for it is with the heart that man believes (Rom. 10:10). The heart is the seat of desires; and as one longs for things, those things may actually be drawn in.

In a corresponding fashion, evil may be drawn within through the heart of a person. The Apostle James explained:

> Then when lust has conceived,
> it gives birth to sin; and when
> sin is accomplished, it brings
> forth death (James 1:15).

Rather than the positive hope in God, we are talking here about the evil longings within a person's heart. Those lusts actually draw within a person the evil substance of that which is desired. Those things are conceived or planted within one as seeds, and eventually bring forth sin and death.

We see, then, that the heart of man can draw into it both good or evil. Just as the physical heart in a person's body draws in food and oxygen, and then pumps those nutrients throughout a person's body, so also the spiritual heart of a person draws in spiritual substance and then redistributes it throughout a person's entire life. It is through the heart of man that spiritual substance — good or evil — can pass from the spiritual world into this natural world.

# 10

## Open Doorways for Power to Flow

The extent to which a person serves as a doorway for spiritual things to enter the natural world is determined primarily by the agreement throughout his entire being. When the heart, mind, emotions, and all one's strength are pointed in the same corresponding direction, then there can be a free flowing of spiritual things through that person.

Allow me to give you an example of this principle from my own ministry. For several years, I pastored a church. During that time, I had an associate pastor working with me who was used of God strongly to minister in the spiritual gifts. During the beginning of my ministry at that church, I spoke in tongues, but I did not believe that *all* Christians should speak in tongues. In contrast, my associate pastor believed that every Christian should have this gift from God. In line with our differing beliefs, my associate and I had two different results in our ministries when we prayed over people to receive this gift. I noticed that almost every person he prayed over would receive this work of the Holy Spirit quickly and begin speaking in other languages. When I prayed over people, they would seldom receive the gift of tongues. The results we saw were according to our different beliefs.

This changed in time. One day my associate pastor was talking to me about the gifts of the Holy Spirit, and he convinced me that day that all Christians can have this gift if they desire it. Something changed within me at that moment. It was as if a switch flipped on. I believed 100% as he did. My beliefs and thinking came into full agreement. As a consequence, my ministry changed. A greater flow was opened through me that day.

There are even more obvious examples about which we can talk, involving the release of spiritual power through a person. In some cases, the heart of a person can be fixed open to such a degree that some spiritual substance seems to flow through in an unhindered manner. We call a person in this condition an "open doorway."

**open doorway**

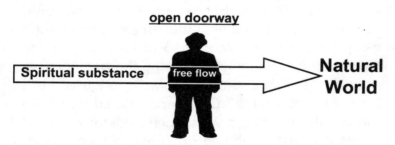

Spiritual substance — free flow → **Natural World**

Some people have given themselves over to evil practices and beliefs to such a degree that they have become open doorways. As a consequence, spiritual energy corresponding to Satan's desires may flow through them, which influences other people in a negative way.

For example, there are people deeply involved in the homosexual culture who believe 100% in what they are doing. Their thoughts, desires, and entire being have been conformed to the related evils. Those spiritual energies not only influence that individual, but they may flow through him and "spill" out onto others nearby.

A prime example of people serving as open doorways is portrayed by those who walk on blistering hot coals without being burned. This has been practiced by several different sects around the world, but perhaps the most amazing is a group living in Surinam (Dutch Guiana). They have an annual religious ceremony, during which the men of the tribe practice a dance amidst flames reaching to their waists. During that dance, they are barefoot and have no protection from the heat. Afterward, those involved show absolutely no burns or blisters anywhere on their bodies.

The spiritual part of this ceremony is evident as a woman of the tribe, called the virgin priestess, goes into a trance (under the influence of a devil). Only as long as she remains in this trance do the men continue dancing in the fire. When her trance-like state passes, the men immediately get out of the fire to avoid being seriously burned.

priestess in a trance

We could talk about a similar supernatural occurrence worked by God. In the book of Daniel, we read about Shadrach, Meshach and Abednego being thrown into a blazing furnace. Though the soldiers who threw them in were burned to death, the three men of God were unharmed while walking about in the midst of the flames (Dan. 3:19-30). We would explain this by saying that God reached out of the spiritual realm and intervened, holding back the natural laws which normally would have acted upon those men.

We can learn of other open doors between the spiritual and natural world by talking about evil mediums who contact the dead. Certain mediums have been known to put themselves into trance-like states, and in that condition, spirit entities are allowed to flow through them so as to manifest in some way in the natural world.

Similarly, there are people used as *channelers* today. A channeler is someone who completely yields himself or herself to a spirit entity (a devil), so that it may speak freely through him or her. Of course, those calling themselves channelers do not admit that devils are speaking through them. Instead, they claim dead people or some wise spiritual being is communicating through them. As Christians, however, we know that such communication is forbidden (Deut. 18:10-12) and is demonic in origin.

We could contrast this with the Christian practice of prophesying. When the Holy Spirit comes upon a Christian, he or she may begin to speak out a message from God. What makes this Christian practice good and the channeler's practice evil is the *source*. Both yield themselves to spirit beings, but God speaks through the believer.

However, we must not include all prophesying under the category of open doors. The terminology *open door* is not a Biblical term. It is simply a descriptive label we use to help us understand the total and complete yielding of oneself, so that the free flowing of some spiritual substance is possible. When Christians prophesy, there are times when they yield in a full open-door fashion, but there are other occasions when a much more restricted flow moves through them.

Some people functioning as open doors seem to go into trance-like states. Others maintain an awareness of everything going on, but they seem to be uninvolved in the activity.

For example, consider the ministry of Kathryn Kuhlman. While she was alive, she typically would teach in her meetings for an hour or so, and then the Holy Spirit would begin manifesting in such a way that people were physically healed. In the most powerful services, she did not lay her hands on people to pray for them. Instead, the power of God seemed to fill the whole room, and she simply would watch the miracles happen and point them out to the audience. In her own explanations, she would describe how she felt uninvolved — as if she were standing at a distance, simply watching herself move and act.

In addition to healing power, there are other aspects of God's nature that can flow through a person. Certain anointed worship leaders seem to be able to open heaven so that the presence of God falls. Many different ministers have been used by God for conviction power and holiness to flow through them. For example, when Charles Finney was alive, the convicting power of God often would flow through him so strongly that people would cry out in anguish of soul. There have been times in Leonard Ravenhill's ministry when the fear of God poured into the atmosphere and everyone present came under its influence. Other Christians have been used to bring joy and laughter to God's people. Some leaders have been used of God as doorways for a spirit of liberality to come upon the people so that all those present wanted to give away everything they owned to help others. I also have been in meetings where it seemed as though heaven opened and visions of the last days were upon us. In each case God has used a person at the front to "open the windows of heaven" to release some aspect of His nature into the natural world.

A doorway to the spiritual realm becomes locked open within a person as he comes into full and complete agreement throughout his entire being. It is not just the casual believer who becomes an open doorway. Some people come to such wholehearted beliefs throughout their beings, almost as if faith and confidence were given to them at birth. Others receive the ability as God touches them at some point during their life. Most people pay a high price before attaining such a state. Some have had to suffer or be put in extreme circumstances where they "had to believe." Others simply have continued believing in some particular fashion for a long period of time, and gradually their entire being came into conformity to that specific way of thinking. Pressure, trials, suffering, extended difficulties, continual exposure, etc., are often the environments through which a person is formed into an open doorway.

The conditions of an open door also may be the results of a group dynamic. In such cases, it is not just the single leader up front who opens the door to the spirit, but many people in agreement with that leader function together to create the conditions.

For example, James Steward was a powerfully anointed evangelist who ministered primarily in Europe. On one occasion, it was reported that the presence of God descended upon a large congregation and a holy hush came over the meeting. At the end, when everyone was dismissed, they all left quietly without anyone saying a word. So captivating was the presence that no one dared to start the motors in their automobiles, lest they violate the holy presence. All the people walked away that night, leaving their cars in the parking lot.

What was going on behind the scenes of James Steward's meeting? A team of intercessors had privately gathered in another room and were reaching into the throne room of God through prayer and focused attention. They formed a united team for the nature of God to flow through James Steward and to the people. They were united with him in faith as an open doorway.

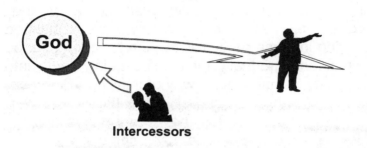

**Intercessors**

Relate these principles to the words of our Lord in Matthew 18:20:

> "For where two or three have
> gathered together in My name,
> there I am in their midst."

In the context of this verse, Jesus was teaching His disciples about binding or loosing His power. We must realize that binding and loosing involves a total and complete agreement of people concerning one thing. It is not just a casual prayer. Nor does it happen in the normal gathering of Christians. Of course, God is present, *in spirit*, whenever Christians come together. But this verse is promising us much more than His invisible, unknowable presence. Jesus said He actually and literally would come — that is, *manifest* — whenever two or more believers come into full agreement. This is that to which we have been referring as the open door condition.

Those who come into agreement may be a team of prayer warriors. At other times, it is the listeners themselves. Some leaders have the ability to draw everyone present into unity of heart and mind. As people become captivated by the words of a single person at the front, at times they may draw upon him to such an extent that they become the ones who open the door to the spirit through him. In any other environment that leader could not function as a doorway for God's blessings to flow, but when people are longing with everything in their beings, then the individual in focus may become the door.

**Spiritual Blessings**          **United Listeners**

Many people used as open doorways will explain that they feel supernaturally guided. We do not want to make this sound too controlling, or as if a person is unable to stop a certain spiritual manifestation. That is usually not the case. In First Corinthians 14:32, Paul explained that even the spirits of prophets remain subject to the prophets. Any person who is being used powerfully by God could stop it if he or she chose to. (There are some exceptions, because God is sovereign: i.e., Luke 1:20-22.) God usually does not force Himself upon an individual. In contrast, an evil person may give himself over to Satan so many times and to such a degree that he no longer can control himself. When speaking of God's power, we understand that Christians *yield control,* rather than *lose control.* That distinction is important. Anyone can decide to stop if they so choose. However, they also can choose to continue to yield, and God does guide them strongly.

At this point, before closing our discussion of open doors, we should mention a characteristic seen in the lives of many leaders so exercised. People used as open doorways are sometime so focused in their particular field of endeavor that they become unbalanced and extreme. In Church history we read about certain leaders powerfully used of God to accomplish great tasks, while at the same time being blind to other truths. Some powerfully used missionaries have become fixated on visions of people going to hell and how they can lead the lost to Christ. Certain healing evangelists in the middle of the twentieth century seemed to consider healing the only thing important in the Christian experience. There have been many believers with a prophetic passion for some area of ministry, and in their extreme emphasis, we would have to admit that they were not balanced doctrinally, nor were they giving the whole picture of Biblical truth.

In some cases, it is perhaps their extreme nature which has enabled them to be focused enough to accomplish what they did. In saying this, we are not making excuses for those with extreme positions or doctrines. Rather, we simply are trying to understand those in the Body of Christ who have been powerfully used by God. It is in this light that we can understand and accept them.

It is also true that some of the most anointed individuals used in releasing spiritual power have had personal, marital, or financial problems. They have so focused their thoughts and affections on the fulfillment of one goal, that they have neglected other areas of their lives. This is simply inexcusable. People totally focused upon one area have a tendency to become blind. Sooner or later, the areas which they have neglected seem to rise up and destroy them. It is our belief that this is neither necessary nor excusable. Believers can walk in power while maintaining Christian standards in all areas of their lives.

# 11

## Cautions Concerning Spiritual Experiences

Now that we have explained some fundamental principles pertaining to our relationship with the spiritual realm, we want to add a few cautions, warnings, and proper perspectives. These additions will offer further enlightenment on spiritual dynamics. Allow me to address four issues here.

First of all, we must point out that the truths thus far discussed cannot be applied like formulas. For example, we have explained how men can serve as doorways for the spiritual world to influence the natural world; however, this must not be seen as a mechanical function. Overriding all spiritual dynamics is God. The Bible declares Him as "the God of the spirits of all flesh" (i.e., Num. 16:22;27:16). He is a sovereign Lord. For this reason, Christianity cannot be reduced to a list of spiritual mechanics or exercises. God is a Person. He deals with His people as children. He does not allow His children to tap into spiritual powers and just use them as they will. Just because a Christian focuses and opens his spirit does not mean he will receive that which he desires. It is not that mechanical. < God desires relationship, and He is working with us as individuals whom He loves >

A correlation can be made on the evil side. There are witches, clairvoyants, yogis, and other spiritual practitioners who major in the mechanics of releasing supernatural powers. They know how to focus and open themselves to the spiritual realm. In addition, there are others more deeply involved in evil, who actually develop *relationships* with devils. Two different groups of people are seen in super-natural evil practices, although individuals in the first group typically find themselves in the second group after a short time.

In a comparative way, there are Christians who will attempt to apply spiritual principles without a deep relationship with God. They may experience some measure of power simply because God has given man authority to loose spiritual things into this earth. However, God demands more. On judgment day many will stand before our Lord and say, "Lord, Lord, did we not prophesy in Your name, and in Your name cast out demons, and in your name perform many miracles?" And then Jesus will say to them, "I never knew you; depart from Me, you who practice lawlessness" (Matt. 7:22-23). These words carry eternal weight, and the warning must be clear: spiritual power without relationship is not an option. Therefore, as we continue to teach principles related to spiritual powers, we must never lose sight of God, who is the Lord.

A second caution we need to state here relates to the care needed with all spiritual demonstrations. The Apostle Paul explained that spiritual things only can be communicated with spiritual words. Furthermore, he wrote that spiritual expressions are foolishness to the natural mind (I Cor. 2:12-14). Because spiritual things cannot be understood or accepted by those naturally minded, we must choose carefully both the environment and the manner in which they are demonstrated and communicated.

This truth should be united with the fact that every manifestation of the spiritual into the natural involves, to some degree, the person yielding himself or herself to that influence.

For example, consider even the simple manifestation of speaking with other tongues as described in the Bible. Today, when Christians receive this gift they must yield a part of their own being to the control of the Holy Spirit. If they are unwilling to yield, then they will be unable to receive this gift. Some Christians have prayed for this gift, but have not received because they want to maintain control of their own thoughts and the words coming out of their mouth. The Apostle Paul explained that with this gift the mind of the person is "unfruitful" (I Cor. 14:14). Therefore, in order to receive this gift the recipient must yield control, in the sense of letting things flow unhindered by the human mind. I have learned through experience that in order to receive the gift of tongues, people often must be encouraged to "loosen up and let go". As long as they are stiff and in control, they are hindering the flow. They are not yielding. In the Book of Acts we read how bystanders on the day of Pentecost thought the early disciples were drunk with wine (Acts 2:15). The disciples were acting loose and unhindered. In a similar fashion, people today must *come under the influence* of the Holy Spirit before they *receive* His influence.

So also with the more powerful spiritual manifestations. There are some workings of the spiritual dimension which flow into a person and simply enlighten his or her own thoughts and desires. But there are others, especially those involving open doorways, which require a yielding to a much fuller extent. These can manifest in the life of the individual in demonstrations which seem foolish to the natural mind.

For example, the prophets in the Bible often "acted out" the very principles they were relaying from the spiritual dimension. Isaiah walked around publicly naked and barefoot at the command of the Lord (Is. 20:2-3). Ezekiel laid on the streets of Jerusalem for over a year (Ezek. 4). The Prophet Agabus in the New Testament bound his own hands with a belt in order to demonstrate what later would happen to Paul (Acts 21:10-14).

Even today, we see people who are tapped into the spiritual dimension sometime being caught in spiritual symbolism or expressions. Intercessors may curl up and groan as they pray, much like Elijah did when he prayed for rain (I Kings 18:42). Some people may fall to the ground unable to move, as John did when he saw the Lord (Rev. 1:17). When people are releasing spiritual things into the natural world, the words, expressions, and behaviors they show may seem foolish or overly exaggerated to our natural mind.

We need to realize that spiritual expressions *not only correlate* with what is going on in the spiritual world, but *sometime they are required for the release of the related powers.* For example, the Prophet Elisha instructed the King of Israel to strike the ground with an arrow; afterward, the prophet explained that the number of times he struck the ground activated God's will for the number of times he would strike down his enemies (II King 13:18-19).

Now, in pointing out the role and the need for spiritual expressions, we are not making excuses for religious nuts or weirdoes who want to attract attention to themselves or justify their bizarre behaviors. In giving the Corinthian Church advice concerning the spiritual manifestations, Paul told them to be mature in all such expressions and not to offend others. Some spiritually-oriented people may try to make excuses for their own obnoxious or unacceptable behaviors, but Paul made it clear that all spiritual expressions are subject to the individual (I Cor. 14:20-33). We are not out of control. All spiritual expressions must be done in a manner and in an environment where they will edify the Church.

This caution is given not just for the benefit of the whole Church, but also for the protection of the spiritually-oriented person. Because the spiritual things may be foolish to the natural mind — and they are often personal and intimate revelations not understood by others — one should be careful with whom he shares them. Jesus explained to His disciples that they should not cast their pearls before swine, lest they be trampled under foot (Matt 7:6). People who share "all their pearls" find that others have a difficult time accepting any kind of ministry from them. Observers even may ridicule to the extent of wounds being inflicted. Those who are spiritually oriented need others with whom they can share things, for the purpose of discernment and understanding. However, spiritual things must be discussed in the presence of mature Christians who are able to discern things spiritually (I Cor. 2:14-16).

A third caution has to do with the *sensation of mastery* sometime experienced by those tapped into the spirit. When a person detaches from this world's thoughts and concerns, he or she may feel free and "above" this world. It can be as if they are looking down on life, problems, and everyone else. They may feel a sense of superiority. All other people may seem inferior — less enlightened.

It is true that certain things can be known by tapping into the spirit, but it is also true that deception very often creeps into the minds of those who are only spirit-oriented. As we explained, those who are not grounded in natural reality and in real relationships with other people begin to float and drift on the waves of spiritual energy. Also, the imagination and desires of the individual influence the spiritual world. That which is desired easily forms in spiritual visions. Because of this, it is difficult to separate what is actually in the spiritual realm from what has taken form through the thoughts and desires of the person.

More will be taught in later volumes concerning the dangers of using spiritual power, but here we can point to the root evil of pride. Knowledge makes arrogant (I Cor. 8:1). Whether that knowledge is true or only a figment of the person's imagination, many spiritually-oriented people have fallen through exalted images of self.

Fourth and finally, in our discussion of warnings and proper perspectives, we want to mention the danger of confusing God with the spiritual world itself.

This error is most obvious among the millions of followers of the Buddhist religion. Devotees are taught to go into the spirit and become "one with the cosmos" — the cosmos being everything in existence. It is believed that if a person devotes his life to escaping the natural realm and fixing his mind on spiritual things, he actually will become a part of those spiritual things. The Buddhist practitioner also believes that God *is* the universe, and therefore, when a person makes himself one with everything, then he is one with God — he is God. That, then, is the goal of the religious elite in the Buddhist faith.

What happens in actual outworking is that a devotee develops a state of mind which is detached from this world. He will deny all natural desires and attempt to empty himself completely. No thoughts. He achieves an altered state of consciousness where he is not aware of most things going on in this world, but is unattached, mystical, and distant. He then has arrived, he believes, at divinity.

Notice the error at the very foundation of Buddhist thought. They believe that God *is* the cosmos, or that He *is* the spiritual realm. They think they are encountering God when, in actuality, they are experiencing detachment from natural responsibilities and thoughts.

It is true that detachment from this world may leave one with a carefree, above-all, relaxed feeling. But that feeling is not God. God is a Person who exists in the spiritual realm. He is not the spiritual realm, but He is the Person who rules there. A person can go into the spiritual realm and not experience God. He may, like the Buddhist, confuse God with the experience of the spiritual dimension.

This Eastern way of thinking also pervades New Age thought. New Age practitioners do not know the difference between God and the spiritual realm. They think God is the spiritual realm, and when they experience the spiritual realm they conclude they are experiencing God.

This deception even can creep into the lives of devoted, sincere Christians. As we explained in an earlier chapter, some people, in their earnest desire to live right before God, will develop a lifestyle of being mystical and detached from this natural world. They may keep themselves in an altered state of consciousness and even walk around with a glazed-over look in their eyes. Combine this deception with the previous warning we gave concerning people feeling a sense of mastery as they tap into the spirit. It can be difficult to deal with people so deceived, because they think they are above and superior to everyone else. At the root of those individuals' belief is the lie that God *is* the spiritual realm. They think they are in tune with God because they are keeping their consciousness open to the spiritual dimension.

Although we must warn the spaced-out Christian who thinks he is walking with God, we still want to acknowledge the experience of God which can be found in the spirit. Whenever a group of Christians gather together and become of one heart and mind, our Lord declared that He would be in their midst (Matt. 18:20). Therefore, we can be reassured that when Christians worship God with all their hearts and minds, He will be present.

As Christians sing songs and turn their hearts toward God, they may detach from all the problems weighing them down. As they enter the spiritual dimension, they may feel free and relaxed. That is good and should be encouraged. However, the believer should be encouraged to go deeper than just the experience of being relaxed. God exists in the spiritual realm. As we draw near to Him, He will draw near to us. Furthermore, the Church is the dwelling place of God. As Christians gather together and focus corporately upon Him, He will make Himself known. He may communicate with individuals, or reveal Himself in many other ways. God comes when Christians seek Him.

In contrast, when non-Christians go into the spiritual realm, they may experience that dimension where they can feel carefree and happy; however, it is not God. They also may tap into some spiritual power. The Christian, on the other hand, has access to God. He should not confuse the experience of the spiritual realm with the Person of God, but he and she can know that God is there.

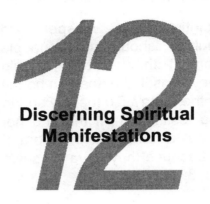

## Discerning Spiritual Manifestations

Perhaps the greatest challenge we face is discerning good from evil. In volumes that follow this chapter, we will be discussing many supernatural and spiritual phenomena. We must go into those discussions with a Biblical understanding of the spiritual world and a basis for discernment. Let's conclude this first volume by providing that basis.

First of all, we must listen to whatever is being taught as various spiritual manifestations are being brought forth. If, indeed, what is being spoken is from God, then it will agree with the written Word of God. Concerning the Bible we are told, "All Scripture is inspired by God and profitable for teaching, for reproof, for correction, for training in righteousness" (II Tim. 3:16). We, therefore, can use the Bible as a standard to judge various spiritual phenomena and manifestations. In the Book of Isaiah, we read the exhortation from God through the prophet:

> And when they say to you,
> "Consult the mediums and the

> spiritists who whisper and
> mutter," should not a people
> consult their God? Should
> they consult the dead on behalf
> of the living? To the law and to
> the testimony! If they do not
> speak according to this word, it
> is because they have no dawn
> (Is. 8:19-20).

Notice that our standard always must be the Word of God. We are never to consult mediums or spiritists, and when any spiritual manifestation is brought before us, we must examine it to see if its message agrees or disagrees with the written Word that God already has given to us.

Our second basis for discernment of good from evil is to observe the results in individuals' lives. Our Lord Jesus taught us that there would be true and false prophets coming into the world, and that we would be able to discern them by watching their fruit (Matt. 7:15-20). He made it clear:

> "A good tree cannot produce
> bad fruit, nor can a bad tree
> produce good fruit" (Matt.
> 7:18).

As things are brought from the spiritual world into the natural, they eventually will produce visible effects in the lives of other people. Some of these effects may take time to reveal themselves, but if we watch patiently, we will see the truth.

Third and last, we must examine spiritual manifestations in respect to their exaltation of Jesus Christ as Lord. In First Corinthians 12:1-3, the Apostle Paul tells us:

> Now concerning spiritual gifts, brethren, I do not want you to be unaware. You know that when you were pagans, you were led astray to the dumb idols, however you were led. Therefore I make known to you, that no one speaking by the Spirit of God says, "Jesus is accursed"; and no one can say, "Jesus is Lord," except by the Holy Spirit.

Notice here that Paul is giving us a basis to judge, so that we will not be led astray. What is that basis? Whenever spiritual power or manifestations are evident, we must look to see who is being glorified. If the power being used is of God, then Jesus Christ will be exalted as Lord. If evil power is being released, then Jesus Christ will not be glorified. Jesus, then, is the basis for true discernment of spiritual power.

This third test has been misunderstood by some people, because they have heard of specific cases which are confusing to them. For example, we know of certain demonically possessed individuals who will say out of their mouth, "Jesus is Lord." However, the Jesus to whom they are referring is not the One who came down from heaven to die for our sins. There are many people named Jesus, especially in countries like Mexico. Those specific individuals certainly are not Lord. When God's power is being used, it is the Jesus Who sits at the right hand of God, Who is being exalted as Lord of all.

Another point of confusion may come when a certain person employs various evil practices, while at the same time incorporating pictures of Jesus or words from the Bible. For example, some Filipino healers are known for carrying out certain mystical healing practices using the cross and other Christian symbols. The use of such Christian emblems or the employment of certain Biblical terms, does not necessarily mean the power they are using is of God.

What we must look for is an actual belief and confession of Jesus as Lord — Lord meaning Number One, Master, Supreme over all.

Jesus taught His disciples concerning this truth. One time they came to Him complaining that there was another man not associated with them, but who was healing people using the name of Jesus. Our Lord's response was surprising to the disciples because He said:

> "Do not hinder him; for he who
> is not against you is for you."
> (Luke 9:50).

Notice that when dealing with spiritual power, it is either for God or against Him. As people use the name of Jesus and truly see His power, they will become more and more convinced concerning Who Jesus truly is. On the other hand, whenever people use demonic power, they become progressively more confused about His Lordship.

One example I can give is from a cultic community where approximately 4,000 people presently are living (at the time of this writing). The leader of this cult is a woman who has been known to heal, at times, various kinds of diseases through the laying on of her hands. One time I was interviewing some people working at this cult center, and I point-bank asked them the question, "Why did Jesus die on the cross?" I can remember the response of the first person: "I have no idea." That answer immediately tells us that the power at work in that cult is demonic rather than of God. However, it is interesting to point out that they still talk about Jesus and think of Him as a great religious leader. They see Him as one of many "Ascended Masters," on a level equal with others like Buddha, Mohammed, etc. Our point of discernment here is that they do not see Jesus as Lord, above all others.

Let me say it again: the more people get involved with demonic power, the more they will become confused concerning Who Jesus Christ is, and in particular, concerning His supreme Lordship over all others.

Now consider our three fundamentals for discernment: (1) agreement with the written Word of God; (2) fruit; and (3) the exaltation of Jesus Christ as Lord. It is vital that Christians today embrace, understand, and apply these.

# Conclusion

To conclude this volume, I would like to emphasize the importance of understanding the spiritual realm and our discussion of the related topics.

The world around us is being exposed to supernatural realities at an amazing rate. Consider the average child growing up in our Western society today. They have heard about astrology, near-death experiences, studies in parapsychology, New Age practices, psychics, voodoo, clairvoyants, alien sightings, people walking on hot burning coals, and other spiritual phenomena. Recently, there has been a tremendous increase of television programs in which there is open discussion of spiritual experiences. The people involved often are embracing spiritual encounters as angelic visitations or God-inspired. There are also numerous documentaries on educational channels explaining the religious rituals of every culture, including primitive third-world peoples using various drugs to tap into the spirit. The average twelve-year old in our modern society has been exposed to religious and spiritual phenomena from all over the world.

Contrast this to the world situation before the 1960's. People lived in much more isolated environments. Most people associated with others in their community who held similar beliefs to their own. Exposure to radically differing views typically was limited to hearing bits and pieces about a culture in another part of the world, or about some distant group of people.

Today, the world is getting smaller in the sense of rapid communication and transportation. Therefore, people who are active in society either must block out the views of others, or incorporate into their thinking the fact that many people around them believe differently than they.

Perhaps the greatest challenge is in the collision of the Eastern world with the West. At no other time in history has this conflict been so real and prevalent. It will be helpful for you to understand this.

The Western mind has been strongly influenced by scientific thought. People in the Western world, therefore, tend to think in terms of cause-and-effect relationships on a natural level: natural things cause natural results. In contrast, people in the Middle and Far East are much more likely to look for spiritual causes to explain the circumstances around them: spiritual things cause natural results. As we state this, we do not want to oversimplify. Some of the greatest scientific minds live in the East. Furthermore, some groups in the West, such as the native American Indians and even certain Christians, especially in Charismatic circles, are very conscious of the spiritual world. However, we are talking here about general patterns of thought which have resulted from the influence of science and naturally based thinking upon the West.

Let me give you an example of this difference. If someone suddenly becomes sick, people raised with the Western mind-set immediately will consider medical treatment, dietary changes, or some other natural solution. In many cultures, especially in the East or primitive areas of the world, the thought patterns are not arranged in this way. Millions of people in the Orient immediately would wonder how they can "balance the energies within them." Some will conclude that they have displeased their ancestors. And others may think that demonic spirits are active. As we explain this, realize that approximately half of the world today tends to think in terms of spiritual things being the primary cause of natural problems.

Because the world presently is being united through art, science, economics, politics, and all forms of communication, the Eastern and Western minds are meeting. The East is being introduced to your children, and not just in the form of a television program picturing a Hindu priest chanting or the medicine man hallucinating. It is presented to them on the detective movie when the professional, experienced police officer gets the tip he needs from a spiritually sensitive bystander. It comes to your child when his or her teacher at school talks about the power of positive thinking. It is there when the "Ninja Turtle" or Samurai hero meditates to discover wisdom. Further, it is coming into every scientific field, such as when acupuncture and holistic medicine are being used in the medical field. The Eastern mind is being presented to you in ways of which you are not even aware.

For most people, there is a subtle conflict between the two ways of thinking. The Western mind tends to think of spiritually-aware people as uneducated, primitive, superstitious, mystical, and/or ignorant. On the other hand, those with a more Eastern way of thinking may consider the naturally-based person to be unenlightened and blind to spiritual realities. The first group scoffs and laughs, while the second group holds itself separate and aloof.

You will have to be open to both ways of thinking in order to discover truth. In successive volumes,we will discuss phenomena unfamiliar to us by offering both natural and spiritual explanations. True Christianity is not limited to either way of thinking. The Bible was not written only to those with a Western mind-set. Furthermore, the world around us is now opening to both ways of thinking.

As people in the West are exposed to spiritual realities, they must be taught how to discern that which is good and that which is evil. Those in the East also must find a basis for true discernment. Our position is not as some Christians, who would condemn all that is spiritual and label it as fake or demonic. No. We want to develop a Biblically-accurate view of the spiritual realm and a basis to discern good and evil. As we do this, we will apply these truths to help us understand the spiritual phenomena being reported around us. This is our goal.

This goal is no small task.

The Church presently is facing a great challenge. Almost every religious view in the world has supernatural and spiritual experiences at its foundation. As these things are being brought to those around us, we must be there with answers. The questions in the minds of non-Christians around us are of a nature entirely different from those questions addressed in previous generations. The people who sat next to you in church last Sunday were watching supernatural encounters on their television Saturday evening. Your children are wondering why Joey at school always wears a black cross. It is time we speak about these things. How, as a Christian, am I supposed to view and understand acupuncture? Holistic medicine? Aliens? Psychics? Astrology? Reports of angelic visitations and near-death experiences? Parapsychology? Dreams? Visions? Various forms of meditation? Experiences in the spiritual realm? Your and my personal encounters with the other side?

In this first volume, we have depicted an invisible, spiritual realm where two kingdoms exist: God's and Satan's. Both good and evil exist in the spiritual realm. We have explained in this volume how people receive information from the spiritual realm, and how they can act as doorways for spiritual things to enter this natural world. Finally, we have laid out a Biblical basis for discernment.

We will build upon these foundations in the volumes which follow.

# What is your question?

Although several volumes of this series already have been released, there are later volumes at various stages of completion. If you have questions related to the spiritual realm which you wish to have answered, feel free to submit your questions to our office, and we will consider addressing them in future volumes. We would love to hear from you.

Winepress Publishing
P.O. Box 10653
Yakima, WA, 98909-1653, USA

Or E-mail to: winepress@nwinfo.net

## Books by Harold R. Eberle, available from Winepress Publishing, include the following:

**Spiritual Realities**
Volume I: The Spiritual World and How We Access It
Volume II: The Breath of God in Us
Volume III: Escaping Dualism
(Volumes IV-VII are in various stages of completion)

**Developing a Prosperous Soul**
Volume I: How to Overcome a Poverty Mind-set
Volume II: How to Walk in God's Financial Blessings

**The Complete Wineskin\*** (Restructuring the Church for the Outpouring of the Holy Spirit)
**The Living Sword** (Applying the Word of God to Current Controversial Issues, such as Women in Ministry, Divorce and Remarriage, etc.)
**Two Become One\*** (Releasing God's Power for Romance, Sexual Freedom and Blessings in Marriage)
**God's Leaders For Tomorrow's World** (Understanding Leadership Dynamics, Dealing with Power Struggles and Developing Personal Leadership Abilities)

\*Also available as an audiobook on cassette tape.

For current prices or to place an order by phone, call: **1-800-308-5837** within the USA or **509-308-5837** from outside the USA (MasterCard/VISA accepted).

Winepress Publishing
P.O. Box 10653, Yakima, WA 98989-10653, USA

E-mail: winepress@nwinfo.net
http://www.grmi.org/ministry/winepress/